# ADVANCE PRAISE

"This is the conversation many women have quietly been waiting to hear out loud. We've built remarkable companies, yet too often at the expense of ourselves—and that was never the real goal. When leadership becomes aligned and supported, success stops feeling heavy and finally starts working for your life."

**—Betty Hines**
Founder & CEO Women Elevating Women LLC;
Chair, Women Presidents Organization (WPO) Platinum III;
WPO Global Board of Directors

"*Impossible Freedom* gives language and relief to women who have built extraordinary businesses while burning themselves out. It dismantles the false belief that growth requires self-sacrifice and shows what becomes possible when success and personal well-being are designed to coexist. If you look successful on the outside but feel trapped on the inside, this book is for you."

**—Shea H. Murtaugh**
CEO, Hoffmann Murtaugh, an integrated marketing agency

"After building, scaling, and exiting companies, I found myself asking a deeper question: What kind of freedom do I want now? And who am I beyond what I've built? This book helped me shape my next chapter with intention rather than blind ambition and with a deeper sense of worth beyond output."

**—Coco Sellman**
5x Founder, CEO, Impact Investor

"A profitable business that leaves you perpetually exhausted and misaligned with your own life is no one's vision of true success. *Impossible Freedom* provides powerful tools that shift emphasis from daily reactive crises to value-aligned productivity, allowing business owners the mindset to leverage their teams and time for a life they will embrace."

**—Scott Armstrong**
Owner, Mind Switching Training Inc.

"*Impossible Freedom* clearly put words to the pressure, ambition, and quiet exhaustion so many leaders carry. Nadine and Derek blend honesty, compassion, and real strategy to show that it's completely possible to grow a thriving business without sacrificing yourself in the process. I recommend this book for every striving business owner as the roadmap to realizing that freedom isn't a someday goal—it's something we can choose and build right now."

**—Lynda Bishop**
National Association of Women Business Owners (NAWBO)
Institute for Entrepreneurial Development

"In *Impossible Freedom*, Nadine and Derek name a reality many high-achieving women leaders quietly experience, the 'Middle Zone of Success,' where the business is thriving, but the personal cost is too high. They challenge the long-held belief that sacrifice is simply the price of success and, instead, offer a practical, grounded roadmap for aligning your time, strengthening your team, and making braver leadership decisions rooted in self-trust. This is a powerful guide for CEOs ready to grow their companies without sacrificing their energy, presence, or joy, and redefine success on their own terms."

**—Allison Tabor**, CPC
Women Presidents Organization (WPO) facilitator,
author of *Work Your Assets Off*®: *Stop Working So Hard in Business and In Life*

"This book does something incredibly rare. It paves the pathway for entrepreneurs to finally accomplish something few ever achieve, the ultimate entrepreneurial dream, a true freedom-based lifestyle. If you're an entrepreneur who started your business for freedom (the real kind), this book will change the trajectory of your professional pursuits moving forward—and maybe your family life, your financial life, and your spiritual life, too."

**—Julie Cabezas**
Founder, Self Made

"One of the hardest (and most powerful) things in life is seeing beyond our familiar "can'ts" and finding new possibilities we've been conditioned to overlook. Too many of us never find the right challengers who can help us do this. This book can be your challenger. Nadine and Derek Nicholson don't just expand your sense of what's possible, they guide you toward the brave, necessary action to create it."

**—Lisa Haggis**
Founder, Realize Your Brand

"This book shares hard-won truths from real life, not theory. *Impossible Freedom* names what so many leaders feel but rarely say out loud. It offers a wise, honest, and immediately useful roadmap to reclaim your time, your energy, and your life so you have true success. *Impossible Freedom* shows how Nadine and Derek forged these strategies in their day-to-day life in their partnership, their family, and their business. They're the real deal and so is this book."

**—Tracey Trottenberg-Kansas** and **George P. Kansas**
Language and Leadership Mentors,
Co-Founders of Amazing International, Inc.

IMPOSSIBLE
Freedom

Grow a Business
That Fuels Your Life,
Not Consumes It

# IMPOSSIBLE
## *Freedom*

## NADINE AND DEREK
## NICHOLSON

Foreword by Camille Burns, CEO
Women Presidents Organization

Peacock Proud
PRESS

For Keane,

Being your parents has been the greatest privilege of our lives. You are why we stopped waiting for "someday" and started living now. We hope these pages remind you that feeling fully lit up and alive in your one precious life happens one brave decision at a time.

Love,
Mom and Dad

"The meaning of life is just to be alive. It's so plain and so obvious and so simple. And yet everybody rushes around in a great panic as if it were necessary to achieve something beyond themselves."

**—Alan Watts**
*The Culture of Counter-Culture*

# TABLE OF CONTENTS



## PART 1

## THE FOUNDATIONS OF IMPOSSIBLE FREEDOM

CHAPTER 1

## CHAPTER 2

### TIME MASTERY: THE FOUNDATION OF FREEDOM



## CHAPTER 3

### UNITED TEAM: SUPPORT THAT MOVES MOUNTAINS



## PART 2

## LEADERSHIP AMPLIFIERS

## CHAPTER 4

### WILD WISDOM: YOUR INNER COMPASS



## CHAPTER 5

### BRAVE DECISIONS: CONFIDENCE IN MOTION

## CHAPTER 6

## COURAGEOUS CONVERSATIONS: THE POWER OF CONNECTION



## PART 3

## EXPERIENCE IMPOSSIBLE FREEDOM

## CHAPTER 7

## CRAFTING *YOUR* VISION OF IMPOSSIBLE FREEDOM: ASCENDED POSSIBILITY AND SELF-LEADERSHIP



## CHAPTER 8

## DEFYING CAN'T: FROM LIMITING BELIEFS TO LIMITLESS POTENTIAL

CHAPTER 9

**NOT SOMEDAY, NOW: LIVING IN FREEDOM AND LEGACY** . . 177

# FOREWORD

I've spent nearly three decades working alongside some of the most extraordinary and accomplished women in business: founders, presidents, and CEOs building and running multimillion-dollar companies across the globe. Their achievements are remarkable. But behind the metrics, milestones, and awards, most of these leaders are running on empty. As CEO of the Women Presidents Organization (WPO), a global peer-learning community of high-growth, women-led companies, I see this pattern daily—visionary leaders fueling economies, creating jobs, and changing industries while quietly questioning how much longer they can keep holding it all together. They're stuck in a success story that looks amazing on paper but feels unsustainable for them personally.

That's why *Impossible Freedom* matters so much. It puts into words what many have felt but never fully named: that we've been taught to lead in a way that's unsustainable, and that it feels *impossible* to drive business growth while also living a rich, fulfilling life, without having to compromise one for the other.

This isn't just another book wrapped in productivity tools, work-life balance tips, surface-level self-care checklists, or cheerleading from the sidelines. This book is a wake-up call—and a leadership revolution. Nadine and Derek Nicholson of Ascend Leadership Co. offer leaders, especially women who give so much of themselves to their businesses, the permission to reject the trade-offs that many of us have been conditioned to accept. They don't just tell you it's *possible* to grow and scale a business without losing yourself in the process. They *show you how* with practical, real-world, hard-earned strategies and insights.

I first met Nadine and Derek through our shared work supporting entrepreneurs. I was immediately struck by the clarity, expertise, and generosity they bring to their executive leadership coaching. Nadine, the Time Architect and a WPO member, has a gift for seeing and naming truths that leaders may have sensed but never fully articulated or allowed. Derek, the Team Architect, brings a steady, grounding presence that makes sustainable transformation not only possible but inevitable. Together, they embody the partnership they champion and model what it looks like to build a sustainable business that supports your life rather than consumes it.

One of the concepts in this book that resonated most deeply with me is the "Middle Zone of Success." This is the painful plateau where you appear outwardly successful but feel inwardly trapped. Your business may be impressive, but *you* are overextended, overwhelmed, feeling alone, and wondering how much longer you can keep it up. I've seen countless women business owners wrestle with this tension. They've reached the milestones they dreamed of, but the personal cost has been steep: long hours, health concerns, relationship tensions, and very little time for themselves.

Nadine and Derek introduce the "Impossible Freedom Equation" as the way out. It doesn't ask you to push harder, do more, or meditate your way through the chaos. Quite the opposite. It offers a new way of thinking about leadership, one that begins with facing the truth. While reaching your current level of success has taken tremendous dedication, the way you're leading is no longer sustainable. The strategies that got you here won't get you further, and working harder will only keep you stuck.

This book gives you the blueprint to realign. To close the gap between what you say matters and how you actually spend your time. To stop carrying every burden yourself and build the kind of support that sustains growth. To create both financial growth *and* personal freedom, without having to make trade-offs between the two.

The stories in these pages are powerful proof of what's possible. You'll meet women who made brave changes, not because their businesses were failing, but because they refused to settle for business success at the cost of their own lives. These women cut their workweeks in half while doubling revenue. They stopped equating busyness with their worth and stopped feeling guilty when out of the office. They made difficult and complex decisions with precision, finally giving themselves permission to lead differently. Their results are impressive, but even more compelling is the way they describe feeling peaceful, more present, more themselves.

This book also shatters the myth that many leaders mistakenly hold: the belief that more personal freedom will come someday. After the next big project. After the next hire. After achieving the next revenue milestone. After managing the next crisis. Nadine and Derek remind us that your freedom is not something to wait for. There's no perfect time. It's something you choose to claim and make possible *now*, through intentional choices and self-leadership. Not someday. Not later. Now.

For women accustomed to giving endlessly to their businesses, teams, and families, this book's message is both radical and deeply necessary. It reframes leadership not as self-sacrifice, but as self-alignment. It argues that investing in yourself is not indulgent. It's strategic. You are your number one asset, and without your clarity, your energy, and your vision, nothing else can thrive.

*Impossible Freedom* is a lifeline, and I recommend this book wholeheartedly. If you're holding on by a thread, if you feel trapped by your own success, if you've stared at your calendar and thought, *I can't keep doing this*, or if you're tired of pretending you're okay, this book is for you. It offers not only a new way of leadership thinking, but also a proven path and practical tools rooted in purpose, alignment, and sustainable growth.

Nadine and Derek show you how to take your life back without risking all you've built in your business. They help you stop surviving success and start living it. They invite you to stop postponing the life you want and step fully into the life you've been working so hard to make possible.

This isn't just another business book for the nightstand. It's a must-read book about authenticity, legacy, and the kind of leadership the world, and *you*, need more of. Impossible Freedom isn't a dream or a future choice—it's a leadership decision. And it's entirely within your reach now, not someday.

**—Camille Burns**
CEO, Women Presidents Organization

# PREFACE

*By Derek Nicholson*

**B**efore we take you on the journey of this book, there's something you need to know about my co-author, wife, co-parent, and business partner, Nadine: She's a force of nature.

From the moment you meet her, it's clear Nadine sees straight into your soul. Fiercely candid yet disarmingly warm, she brings fire, focus, and deep presence into every room she enters. She's a straight shooter: direct and approachable, with pristine listening, sensing, and being. Nadine has a rare gift for blending sharp business acumen and intuitive wisdom, anchored by a protective "mama bear" instinct that makes you feel both safe and challenged in the best way. I'm in awe of how she cuts through limitations, illuminates what's truly possible, and empowers people to actually do what they really want to do but thought they coudn't.

Working alongside Nadine feels like sitting with Mother Earth: grounded and nurturing, yet sharp and laser-focused. As an expert in compassionate truth-telling and courageous conversations, she helps high achievers take back their time, energy, and joy by cutting through the external noise, pressure, and perceived obligations, and guiding them back to what truly matters to them. They reclaim control, alignment, and freedom to significantly improve both their business success *and* personal well-being. Her masterful coaching creates the conditions for radical clarity, brave decisions, strong boundaries, fearless leadership, and sustainable growth.

At sunrise you'll often find Nadine walking, reflecting, and recharging in the forest or by the river near our home in Alberta, Canada. She's always learning, always expanding, always pushing her own edges. Nadine is unwavering in her commitment to helping leaders, especially women, own their time, power, intuition, and vision without apology. For her, real, no-nonsense conversations and clear-eyed action always take precedence over polish or perfection. Nadine is truly a powerhouse.

Together, Nadine and I co-founded Ascend Leadership Co., where we help women founders and CEOs leading seven- to nine-figure businesses drive extraordinary business and financial growth without compromising what matters most to them personally. Through transformational executive leadership coaching and bold strategy, we guide and empower leaders to redefine and create success on their own terms with confidence and profound connection to their own inner wisdom. Our goal is to help you achieve what too many overwhelmed leaders think is impossible today: a business that grows and scales in a way that fuels, rather than consumes, your personal freedom, enabling you to live a fulfilling, joyful life aligned with your true values and priorities. Because real life isn't something to put off for "someday." Life is now, and you deserve to live it fully.

We call this approach to business and life ascending to Impossible Freedom™, meaning you're feeling fully lit up in business and life—*and* driving more financial growth at the same time. The paradox of Impossible Freedom is both radical and natural. Ambitious and easeful. Deeply personal and undeniably strategic. And our own path to Impossible Freedom mirrors how this book came to be.

In 2017 Nadine was running her own leadership development business for entrepreneurs, while I worked in corporate consulting, specializing in leadership coaching and organizational development in the oil and gas and healthcare industries. Her business had grown to the point that it could support our family financially. After years of pushing hard in high-pressure roles, I finally had the chance to pause and take a sabbatical. I embraced the opportunity to be a stay-at-home dad and volunteer at our son Keane's school. But as time went on, I started to feel restless.

One afternoon I found myself standing in our kitchen, the dishwasher freshly emptied—again. I turned to Nadine. "I can only empty the dishwasher so many times," I told her honestly. "I know you appreciate what I do at home, but I miss the feeling of healthy competition at work, of making a difference in a business setting, and just hearing a 'thank-you' from colleagues."

As I explored what might come next for me, I began meeting colleagues for coffee. Those conversations reignited a spark I hadn't felt in a while. I noticed how animated I became when talking shop, and I could see that my network still valued my skills and experience. Meanwhile, Nadine watched all this unfold, and while she supported my happiness, she later admitted feeling a twinge of envy as others tried to recruit me for their ventures.

When a friend offered me a partner position to help grow his corporate leadership consulting business, Nadine asked a question that stopped me in my tracks. "What would it be like for you to join me and put your energy, skills, and expertise into growing my business?"

We had never seriously considered working together before, so the idea felt new and a bit daunting. I needed time to think through what this move would mean for my career, my sense of purpose, our marriage, and our family. We both weighed the options carefully. In the end, we decided to join forces in business.

At the time, Nadine's business was called MeJane, a name that played on "Me, Tarzan" and "You, Jane," helping women entrepreneurs embrace their ambition, tap into their Natural Genius™, and invent bigger possibilities for themselves. But as we began planning how to work side by side, it became clear that the business needed to evolve from "hers" into something that felt like "ours."

To do that, we began the strategic branding work of transforming MeJane into what would become Ascend Leadership Co. The process reminded me of an experience from early in our marriage, when we both owned our own homes. Before we wed, Nadine moved into my house but kept hers as a rental. After a year of living together, Nadine shared that she wanted us to find a new place, somewhere we chose as a couple that belonged to both of us equally, right from the start. I agreed. We sold my house, kept Nadine's house as a rental, and bought a new home for us together.

Co-founding Ascend Leadership Co. was much the same. We wanted to build something that reflected both of us from the ground up. The jungle imagery of MeJane gave way to the Three Sisters Mountains, our new nature totem, symbolizing our home in the Canadian Rockies and our shared vision of leadership and life as a journey upward. Instead of walking parallel paths, we were building something together, learning to rely on each other in new ways and forging a shared future of Impossible Freedom.

Just as Ascend Leadership Co. evolved from Nadine's solo venture into something we co-created and co-owned, Nadine was originally going to write this book alone. After all, she had always been the main spokesperson for the business, championing it and our mission publicly. But over time, as we worked together with clients and defined our individual leadership lanes (Nadine as the Time Architect, helping high achievers reclaim and redesign their time, and me as the Team Architect, helping them build united teams), we realized something important: Our greatest value to the people we serve comes not from working separately, but from bringing our unique perspectives and expertise together. Our clients tell us time and again that it's the combination of Nadine's unapologetic clarity and my steady presence that helps them create lasting, sustainable change. We knew the same would be true for our readers.

That's why this book represents both our voices and lived experiences. By writing it together, we share the depth, insight, and practical tools that have transformed our clients' lives and businesses. Our hope is that the lessons we've learned about aligning your time, strengthening your team, and making braver leadership decisions rooted in self-trust will empower you to climb out of the Middle Zone of Success™, that deceptive plateau where your business and achievements look impressive from the outside, but behind the scenes, you feel overextended, trapped in the day-to-day, and unable to enjoy the very success you've built.

For me, years spent in corporate roles (while leading, coaching, and collaborating with powerhouse women) prepared me for my next chapter supporting women leaders through our work at Ascend Leadership Co. In one of my final corporate positions, I was a senior manager overseeing a 110-person home care team in healthcare, more than a hundred of whom were women. By then, I had built a deep foundation of leadership experience, particularly in healthcare and service-based environments, and I knew exactly how I wanted to lead. My approach was grounded in trust, empathy, and support. I wasn't there to dictate; I was there to empower. My job was to remove obstacles so others could succeed.

That leadership philosophy shaped everything that followed. By focusing on one-to-one connections, job shadowing overnight shifts, and listening deeply, I helped turn a struggling team into the most successful in the hundred-thousand-employee organization—fully staffed, under budget, and a place where people wanted to work. The experience sharpened my ability to manage complexity, navigate union dynamics, and lead high-stakes conversations with clarity and care. Those years in healthcare, an industry led by and built on the contributions of women, shaped my understanding of what it really means to support, challenge, and champion others. I continue learning lessons to become an "integrated" man, confident in *both* my masculine and feminine energy, and fully equipped to help women founders and CEOs thrive.

One pivotal turning point early in my journey came in 2008 during a professional training program for coaches that Nadine and I enrolled in together. The first day I walked into a room full of strangers and watched in awe as many shared openly, listened generously, and supported each other with a kind of emotional honesty I had never seen before. While others leaned in, I felt myself pulling away. The vulnerability in the room made me so uncomfortable, I nearly walked out.

Up until that point, I'd spent most of my life skimming along the surface of human connection—efficient, capable, but emotionally removed. I didn't realize how detached I'd become until I saw what real connection looked like. That moment cracked something open in me. It taught me to listen not only with my head, but with my heart. It showed me how to nurture relationships with presence, not performance. That shift didn't just change how I lead. It changed how I parent, how I partner, and how I live.

Born from a shared calling to help others, this book distills the hard-won lessons Nadine and I have each learned as hyper-independent and high-achieving individuals committed to leading, growing, and building in true partnership. We didn't arrive at Impossible Freedom by accident. We earned it by making difficult decisions, having uncomfortable conversations, and letting go of identities, habits, and beliefs that no longer served us. We designed our lives and business from the inside out—not because it was easy, but because we believed something better was possible.

If you've ever felt stretched thin by your ambition, torn between your business and your personal well-being, or wondered if there's more, this book is for you. You're not alone. And you don't have to choose between achievement and alignment, impact and inner peace, success and self. You can have all of these. You can have Impossible Freedom: when you feel fully lit up in business and life—*and* drive more financial growth at the same time.

This is your invitation to begin.

# INTRODUCTION: THE IMPOSSIBLE FREEDOM EQUATION

*By Nadine Nicholson*

I was sitting in a ballroom, clapping wholeheartedly as a group of trailblazing women were recognized for building some of the highest-growth companies in the world. The award ceremony was electric, a glittering event full of glamor, hugs, and high-wattage smiles. One after another, awards were given to the leaders of extraordinary, multimillion-dollar companies that had landed them on national lists and magazine covers. The energy in the room was buzzing with admiration, pride, and celebration.

But partway through the ceremony, something shifted inside me. As I watched the smiling faces cross the stage, I felt my throat tighten because I personally knew a different version of many of these women's stories. I had spoken with several of the winners earlier that day and couldn't stop thinking about what they had shared with me privately and what I also knew about leaders I met and had worked with over the years.

One leader had recently spent a night in the hospital after forgetting to change her tampon during her menstrual flow. She'd been so caught up in a day of back-to-back meetings and travel that she hadn't noticed the danger signals her body was sending. The resulting infection could have been fatal. Her husband wasn't just upset that she was away from home again; he was scared—scared he might actually lose her. Earlier that week, their son had asked, "Mom, are you okay? I barely see you anymore." She admitted to working sixteen-hour days, pushing her body beyond exhaustion, worried she would die working, and not remembering the last time she spent a weekend without stepping foot in her office.

Another leader shared how she'd grown her company to over $100 million in revenue in only six years, but she hadn't seen her elderly father in months. "I feel like I'm missing out on the last years of his life," she said. "And for what? I don't even have a life outside of work anymore."

A third leader told me her team still depends on her for too much, and she wakes up each day already behind. She described days where she forgets to eat lunch, misses school pickup, and falls asleep with her laptop still open. The rare moments she does step away, like sitting on the porch with a coffee or spending time with her family, are instantly flooded with guilt that she should be working. "I can't relax," she said, "because I know the second I stop, everything will fall apart. And it will be my fault."

Yet another said while she tried to balance family and business and not give up one for the other, she allowed the business to take precedence and let her marriage fall by the wayside. She's now working to rebuild her marriage.

As applause echoed through the ballroom, I felt something rising in me: Grief. Frustration. A hollow ache in my chest.

Yes, these women deserved to be celebrated. They had founded and built remarkable businesses, created jobs, achieved explosive growth. But at what personal cost?

That question became a turning point, not a judgment.

Tears welled up in my eyes. I looked over at my husband and business partner, Derek, sitting next to me. "Are you okay?" he asked. The truth was—no, I wasn't.

I was heartbroken and knew the truth we needed to name out loud.

Because no one in the room was talking about what I knew to be true: that behind most of those brilliant business minds and designer dresses was an untold story of personal sacrifice, stress, and suffering. These women were being honored for their hustle and for building empires, but the toll it was taking on their bodies, their relationships, their joy was going unnoticed or, worse, expected.

That night at the after-party, I pulled aside a friend who had just accepted one of the awards. I was emotional as I shared what I'd been noticing, what I was feeling. She listened, then nodded slowly and said with tears in her eyes, "Nadine, sometimes these awards feel a bit fake. Sure, I'm proud of my company's growth. But I'm literally killing myself doing it."

We stood there, in the middle of the music and the champagne and the congratulations, and my heart hurt again because her story wasn't an exception; it was the norm.

These women—these incredibly capable, passionate, successful women—were being publicly celebrated for business achievements that were privately burning them out. They were getting the growth, the numbers, the press, but not the freedom they thought success would bring.

In fact, their freedom had slipped out of reach. It wasn't gone but hidden beneath the way they were leading.

And I understood it. In many respects, I'd been where they were. I knew the highs of achievement and external validation. It's a thrill being seen, celebrated, and rewarded for pushing hard and delivering results. In my early career, I chased those moments relentlessly, and I was proud of the accolades I earned. They felt like proof that I was doing something right, that I mattered. But beneath the polished surface, I was running on empty. I had been operating from a belief that the path to success required constant trade-offs: long hours, constant availability, sidelined relationships, and a body I treated like a machine. I told myself it was temporary, that the payoff would be worth it. Then I began to see the cost and the possibility of leading differently.

In the weeks after the award ceremony, I reached out to a few more women I had met there. They shared story after story of how they were "crushing it" on paper but crumbling behind the scenes. Some were on the brink of collapse, others already past it. One told me her husband was ill, and she wanted to spend more time at home to be there for him. "I know I need your help to make changes," she said, "but I've got to get through this next business deal first." I hear women postpone making changes like this. They know they want to hire me and Derek to help them, but they put off facing what they know they need to face, usually because they're afraid to do so. They're also more accustomed to prioritizing their businesses over themselves.

This made me think about Pamela Prince-Eason, the CEO of the Women's Business Enterprise National Council (WBENC) and one of the most influential women in the US business world. She had recently delivered a keynote to thousands at her national conference. Just days later she sadly and unexpectedly passed way. Suddenly she was gone.

The tributes flooded in: "So sad." "So sudden." "Life is short." Yes. Life *is* short.

I mention Pamela's sudden passing because I know many women leaders keep postponing the life they say they want for one more quarter, one more acquisition, one more milestone. They keep telling themselves things will get better, and they'll have a chance to breathe later.

But what if later never comes?

Later isn't the answer. Alignment is, and it can start now.

That event in the ballroom changed something in me. I knew that even though I had been standing for women business owners' freedom since 2009, I needed to get louder. I had to tell people the truth—and the alternative: The way entrepreneurs have been taught to chase business success costs too much personally. At Ascend Leadership Co., Derek and I had built a proven model that returns women's freedom *while* they grow. We know women *can* lead radically differently—and without all the personal sacrifice.

## THE PROBLEM: THE MIDDLE ZONE IS COSTING YOU THE LIFE YOU DESERVE

If the stories I've just shared feel painfully familiar, you're not alone. Seeing yourself here is not a failure; it's a doorway. Awareness is the first step out.

I've spent two decades coaching powerhouse women who, like the leaders I met at that award ceremony, are outwardly successful but inwardly depleted. Before we started working together, they built impressive companies, earned accolades, and scaled to heights they once only imagined. And yet, the deeper truth—what surfaces in private conversations and vulnerable moments—is that they were deeply exhausted. They felt trapped in a cycle of constant over-functioning, unsure how to fix it without everything they worked so hard for falling apart.

This is what we call the Middle Zone of Success or Middle Zone™ for short. The Middle Zone is a sign of success because it took you a lot of effort, perseverance, and courage to get there. But it's also a plateau where your business looks impressive from the outside but costs you too much personally on the inside. It's the hidden trap of success without freedom. The frustrating space between the visible success you've built and the personal freedom you deeply crave. A plateau filled with overwork, time guilt, and decision fatigue. While you have an impressive business, you're weighted down by an overloaded calendar, too much responsibility, little time for your own life, and no clear path to lead differently. If you recognize this, you're already at the inflection point.

You're working harder than ever but with diminishing returns. Every decision feels weighty. Every next step demands more of you. And despite all the productivity hacks and leadership strategies you've tried, nothing seems to create real breathing room. Business is like climbing a mountain, and it's harder in the Middle Zone. The strategies that got you here will only keep you here.

You might find yourself living in a state of constant reactivity: putting out fires, fielding too many team questions, saying yes when you want to say no, and grinding through late nights just to stay on top of it all. You might even feel disconnected from, or even resentful of, the very business you once loved. And when you do try to rest or step back, guilt creeps in, convincing you that stepping back will come at a cost you can't afford.

Sometimes the Middle Zone shows up in less obvious ways. Just before Derek and I started writing this book, our family took a long-anticipated trip to Mexico. After experiencing an injury and gaining some weight, I had set a clear intention: to lose the weight and feel strong, healthy, and comfortable in my body. I wanted to show up fully for the vacation and for the season ahead, which was full of exciting client work, public speaking, and book writing. Competing priorities kept winning. I arrived in Mexico at my highest weight ever and felt a deep sense of disappointment. What stung wasn't just how I felt in my body. It was the fact that I had broken a promise to myself.

That fracture in self-trust rippled through both my business and life. For a few months, I found myself holding back. I avoided visibility, second-guessed myself, and showed up to high-stakes opportunities already feeling small. And the impact ran deeper than health or body image. At its core, it was about integrity. And integrity, which means doing what I say I will do, is my number one core value. If I couldn't trust myself to follow through on what mattered to me personally, how could I fully lead with conviction professionally?

That wake-up call was a whisper, one that motivated me to finally lose the weight over the months that followed. The good news is a whisper can be enough to reset your course, and that's the thing about the Middle Zone. It doesn't always roar. Sometimes it whispers, pulling you slightly off course until you wake up one day and barely recognize the way you're living.

That way of living is not sustainable.

Over time it chips away at your energy, your health, your confidence, your creativity. Your *life*. You tell yourself you should feel grateful, and part of you does. But another part is quietly grieving the missed moments, the dreams put on hold, the deep knowing that something isn't right.

This problem is personal for me. I've listened deeply to women just like you. I've heard your frustration, guilt, and shame as you try to explain, sometimes even to yourself, why the life you've worked so hard to create doesn't feel the way you thought it would. I've seen how smart, capable leaders buy into the false belief that endless hustle is a badge of honor. That sacrifice is the price of greatness. That slowing down is indulgent and investing in yourself selfish. Naming the pattern is how you begin to reclaim your power.

I've been there. I've lived that misalignment, and I know there's another way.

Because success without freedom is just survival in a more glamorous outfit.

## THE SOLUTION: REDEFINING SUCCESS AND THE PATH TO IMPOSSIBLE FREEDOM

You've already built something extraordinary, but now you're ready for something more, something higher. Not just more growth, but more space. Not just success, but freedom.

What got you this far won't take you any higher. The strategies that once worked—pushing harder, moving faster, doing more—are now draining you. You've outgrown the old model of leadership, and you're craving a new way forward. One that doesn't demand constant trade-offs between your business and your life.

That's exactly where Impossible Freedom begins.

Impossible Freedom is a radical paradigm shift. It's the leadership breakthrough of having more time, energy, and joy, all while climbing to never-before-seen levels of success. It's the ability to feel fully lit up in business and life—*and* drive more financial growth at the same time. It's what happens when you break free from the Middle Zone and step into a reality where your business serves your life rather than consumes it.

Impossible Freedom means:

- Your time is fully yours again and designed with intention so your calendar reflects what truly matters, not only what's most urgent, and you stay lit up, renewed, and prioritized.
- Your team is united, capable, and committed to driving your vision forward, freeing you from constant reactive management so you're leading what's next, not stuck in what's now.
- You make bold, confident decisions rooted in your inner wisdom and deepest truth so you lead with unwavering self-trust and aren't swayed by "shoulds," external validation, or societal pressures.
- You communicate your needs, ideas, and boundaries with clarity and conviction, saying hard things by being both kind and firm so you create stronger relationships with your team, clients, service providers, and family.

Does this sound too good to be true?

It's not.

Because we've developed the Impossible Freedom Equation™: a proven, step-by-step leadership framework designed specifically for women founders and CEOs like you. This equation is the result of more than three decades of business and leadership experience that Derek and I bring from running multiple eight-figure corporate portfolios, leading large teams, guiding hundreds of powerhouse leaders, and building our own company, Ascend Leadership Co. It's an approach that teaches you how to reclaim your calendar and step away to recharge without guilt, confidently build and lead an engaged team you can rely on, and hit new levels of sales, revenue, and impact with significantly more ease than it took to get you here.

The Impossible Freedom Equation brings together two foundational Leadership Pillars, Time Mastery™ and United Team™, accelerated by three powerful Leadership Amplifiers: Wild Wisdom™, Brave Decisions™, and Courageous Conversations™. These aren't just tools for managing your schedule or delegating more effectively. They transform how you lead your time, team, and business, unlocking a kind of success that uplifts every part of your life.

The Impossible Freedom Equation, as shown in Figure 1, brings together two foundational leadership pillars:

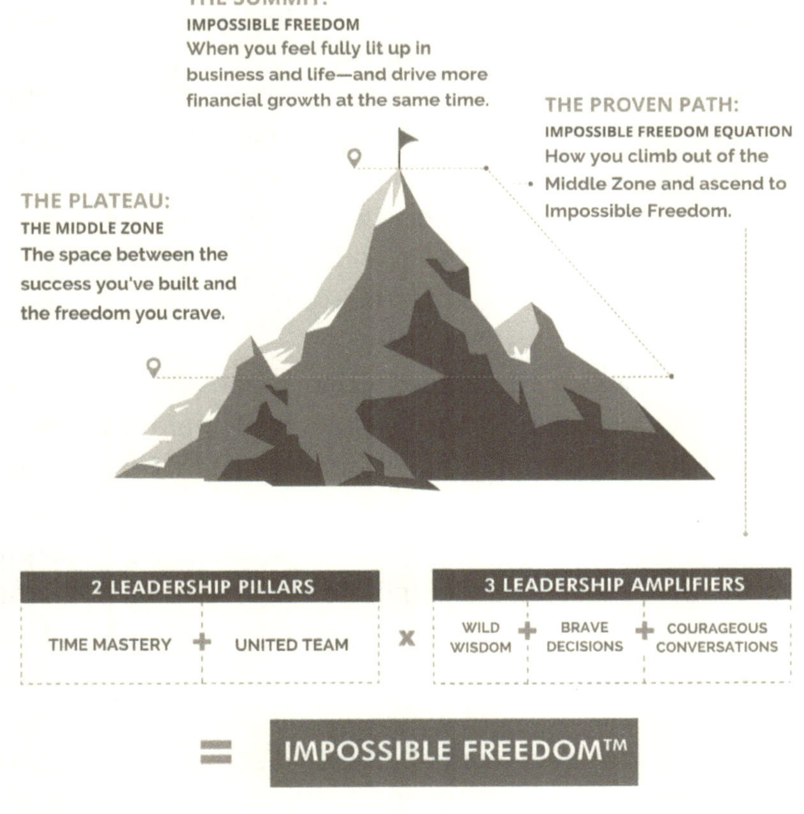


**Figure 1.** The Impossible Freedom Equation.

**Time Mastery:** Bold, unapologetic alignment between what you say matters most and how you actually spend your time. Time Mastery means designing your days with intention so your schedule reflects your values and highest-impact priorities, not just urgent demands. It's about taking ownership of your time, focusing your energy on what you do best so you stay lit up, renewed, and prioritized. Instead of letting external pressures dictate your pace, you create space for what truly matters. The result is your time becomes a source of freedom, fueling both business success and personal fulfillment.

**United Team:** A cohesive, empowered support system that drives your vision forward and frees you to lead strategically, not manage reactively. United Team means surrounding yourself with the right people (employees, partners, mentors, and advisors) who share your mission, contribute meaningfully, and help you lead at the level you're meant for. When your team is aligned and engaged, they carry more of the load, creating sustainable growth for you and your business.

The two core Leadership Pillars are powered by three Leadership Amplifiers:

**Wild Wisdom:** The leadership strategy of trusting your inner knowing (your spirit, intuition, and embodied awareness) so you lead with clarity and self-trust instead of fear. Wild Wisdom reconnects you to your inner compass, helping you move from overthinking to alignment. Being outside in nature is a shortcut to this inner compass. By tuning into the deeper wisdom held in your heart and gut, you can make decisions with confidence, conviction, and calm, even in uncertainty.

**Brave Decisions:** Bold, confident choices rooted in your inner knowing—not external pressure, performance, or "shoulds." Brave Decisions turn clarity into commitment, moving you from insight to action, even when the stakes are high or the outcome uncertain. Practicing Brave Decisions consistently builds momentum, strengthens self-trust, and reinforces the confidence to lead with conviction.

**Courageous Conversations:** Saying the hard things with kindness and firmness, creating connection, accountability, and integrity in every exchange. Speaking openly and honestly about what matters most (your needs, boundaries, ideas, and decisions) builds trust and alignment in every area of life. These conversations strengthen relationships with your team, clients, and family by blending kindness with clarity.

The Impossible Freedom Equation isn't about adding more to your already full plate. It's about changing how you make decisions so your business no longer drains your energy but starts creating the breathing room, impact, and sense of fulfillment you've been craving. Through this model, you'll finally see a way out of the Middle Zone and into a life where your business supports the life you actually want to live. Because the freedom you've dreamed of isn't impossible; it's closer than you think, and it's waiting for you to claim it.

## MEET YOUR GUIDES TO IMPOSSIBLE FREEDOM

### Nadine Nicholson

Hi, I'm Nadine Nicholson—Master Certified Coach, Time Architect, and Chief Possibility Officer at Ascend Leadership Co.

I'm also a wife, mom, nature lover, forest therapy guide, hiking guide, employee communications expert, and fierce believer that real success should give you more life, not less.

For years, I thought the only way to earn success was to work harder than everyone else. I led large teams, advised senior executives, managed multimillion-dollar business operations, and earned international recognition along the way. From the outside, it looked like I had everything I wanted. But on the inside, I was running on empty. Working seventy-hour weeks, I was constantly chasing the next milestone, yet also internally grieving all the moments I missed with my husband, my son, my parents, and myself. My calendar didn't reflect my deepest values. My health and relationships were suffering, and deep down, I knew something had to change.

Then, everything did.

My dad was diagnosed with Stage 4 cancer. Just twenty-one days later, he was gone. In the moment he took his last breath, I felt a surge of clarity, like he had passed on a final life lesson. I saw, in an instant, how out of alignment I was with who and what truly mattered to me, and I made a promise: I would no longer sacrifice my one precious life in the name of success.

That promise became the foundation of MeJane, and then of Ascend Leadership Co. It's the heartbeat of everything I now teach. Today I help powerhouse leaders reclaim their time, energy, and joy so they can lead their businesses and lives with intention, ease, and unapologetic purpose. I coach leaders to return to themselves, to Mother Nature, and to their natural rhythms; to take back control of their calendars; and to make high-impact decisions rooted in their inner truth instead of guilt, fear, or external pressure.

My superpowers? I help women founders and CEOs take back their time, redefine success, and grow their businesses without sacrificing personal freedom or well-being. By staying in touch with my sharp business acumen and heart-centered wisdom, I enable leaders to see the truth of what's *really* going on in their business and their life and then empower and support them to make Brave Decisions and successfully have Courageous Conversations related to that truth. With more than thirty years of guiding and advising senior executives at multi-million and billion-dollar companies, I help leaders cut through the "can'ts" holding them back, illuminate what's truly possible, and guide them to turn their goals and dreams into a reality. I help them focus on *who and what matters most*, so they can stop surviving their success and start living the life they've been dreaming of while making the next decade their best one yet.

Outside the office, you'll find me on a trail in the forest or around Bow River near my home where I reconnect to stillness, wildness, and my own inner wisdom. That's where I find the space to lead, live, and love so that I'm in integrity and alignment with my values. I want you to have your own version of this too.

## Derek Nicholson

Let me introduce you to my partner in life and business, Derek Nicholson—Executive Leadership Coach, Team Architect, Chief Simplicity Officer, and the calm, grounding force behind everything we do at Ascend Leadership Co.

A strategist at heart with impeccably high standards, Derek is the rock you didn't know you needed. Steady and unwavering, he moves through the world with a quiet strength and calm wisdom that draws people in. Whether clearing a path forward in business or guiding a backcountry hike, Derek creates safety, simplicity, and momentum. Keenly observant, curious, and discerning, he sees what others miss. His superpower is cutting through complexity to create practical, solutions. From helping a client navigate a thorny challenge to restructuring a team, Derek brings clarity to chaos and unity to teams. He offers structure without rigidity, clarity without ego, and logic without judgment.

With more than thirty years of experience across industries in leadership development, business scaling, and sales strategy, Derek knows firsthand that a business's success isn't about how hard leaders work, but how effectively they lead. His rare gift lies in staying analytical and focused while remaining deeply heart-centered, making him a powerful and trusted mentor.

Derek helps people lead themselves. He knows that when people feel seen, supported, and clear, everything improves. He helps leaders trust themselves, create buy-in and efficiency within their organizations, and build fully engaged, high-performing teams that operate in their Natural Genius of what they're best at, most passionate about, and what drives more revenue.

He's also a brilliant sales and negotiation coach, guiding clients to amplify revenue through a "relationships-first, always" approach that blends integrity, values, and results. When things feel murky or overwhelming, Derek brings tactical precision. When tough decisions need to be made, he helps you see the right call and make it with confidence. His steady, masculine presence and "special ops" skill set are a mission-critical secret weapon to achieve your biggest goals.

Personally, Derek is my secret weapon and key advisor. When I feel stuck or am emotionally tangled and unsure, he helps me reconnect to my highest truth. He doesn't give me answers; he helps me find my own. Derek is the ultimate sounding board and stabilizing force. He's also a devoted dad and longtime sports coach, mentoring youth in baseball, hockey, and basketball. He plays competitive men's baseball and hockey, and, like me, he recharges in nature. Many of his best ideas come after time spent outdoors breathing in the fresh air.

Most of all, Derek believes leadership isn't something you do—it's a way of being. He lives that belief every day: with integrity, presence, and the quiet confidence that helps everyone around him elevate.

Together, Derek and I are here to guide you through the Impossible Freedom Equation so you can reclaim your time, empower your team, and grow your revenue. Our goal is simple: to help you redefine success that's driven by a set of core beliefs:

- Investing your time into who and what truly matters to you should be the norm, not a radical act.
- Nature offers the fastest path to inner clarity, providing grounding and perspective you won't find behind a desk.
- Real success means feeling happier and healthier by standing in your inner truth and prioritizing the people and experiences that light you up and make you feel alive.
- Family and health come first. Your business should create more time with yourself and loved ones, not take it away.

- The best solutions are often the simplest.
- Comfort zones feel safe, but you were made for growth and bold, courageous leaps.
- Sustainable leadership starts from within. That's why we coach leaders to align their values, mindset, and actions.
- Your dreams and deepest desires deserve follow-through. Intention without execution changes nothing.
- It's time to close the gap between what you say matters and how you spend your time so your life reflects your true priorities.
- You don't need a wake-up call to make a change. Freedom, joy, and fulfillment are available now, not someday.
- Impossible Freedom isn't a dream or future choice. It's a leadership decision. You can drive next-level financial growth and still live the life you truly want. Feeling lit up and fully alive isn't the reward for business success; it's a critical part of achieving it!

## THE JOURNEY WE'LL TAKE YOU ON

This book is designed as a guided ascent that mirrors the climb toward Impossible Freedom itself. Part 1, The Foundations of Impossible Freedom, establishes your foundation by examining the Middle Zone and the Leadership Pillars of Time Mastery and United Team. Part 2, Leadership Amplifiers, propels your progress beyond the Middle Zone through the three Leadership Amplifiers that expand and energize these pillars. Part 3, Experience Impossible Freedom, shifts the focus from understanding Impossible Freedom to embodying it in how you lead and live.

As you move through the chapters, you'll progress from awareness to action, identifying what keeps you stuck, gaining clarity in how you use time and lead your team, and activating the amplifiers that bring greater ease and alignment to your leadership. Each part builds on the last, combining reflection with momentum until freedom becomes not an idea but a lived reality. The journey of this book is designed to mirror your own: a steady climb from recognition to renewed agency and possibility. Our intention is that you feel seen, supported, and strengthened at every step.

Your reading journey begins with recognition. You'll find stories and insights that reflect your own experience—the exhaustion, the overextension, the quiet question of "how much longer can I keep this up?"—with honesty and empathy. This awareness brings relief, replacing isolation with connection and self-criticism with compassion.

As we explore the Impossible Freedom Equation in detail, awareness crystallizes into structured insight. You'll learn to name what's been so difficult to articulate in your leadership, including the gap between what you say and what you do, the limits of the support around you, and the patterns that keep you operating in overdrive without advancing to your next level of business growth. This stage offers structure without judgment, replacing shame with understanding, and gives you the language and clarity you need to reclaim your agency.

From there, the focus shifts to renewal and self-trust. As you discover the three Leadership Amplifiers, you'll learn how to apply them in real time. Emotionally, this is where the journey moves from self-assessment to self-trust. Our role as your guides becomes less about diagnosis and more about possibility, inviting you to see freedom as a natural outcome of leading from self-truth and alignment rather than a reward for working harder.

By the final chapters, insight turns into integration. We'll show you how to translate understanding into practice, crafting your vision, defying limiting beliefs, and sustaining freedom as a daily way of leading and living. By the time you close the last page of this book, you'll have what you need to move forward with clarity, conviction, and readiness, fully invited to act with purpose and confidence.

This is the learning path we promise you: Recognition → Relief → Reflection → Renewal → Readiness. It captures the transformation made possible by the Impossible Freedom Equation: moving from awareness to action, from exhaustion to ease, and from leadership as performance to leadership as presence.

At the end of each chapter, you'll find Reflect to Rise Journal questions. These prompts are invitations to pause, process, and apply what you've learned to your own experience, either with your own or with a trusted circle of peers. You can also download our free *Impossible Freedom Companion* at ascend-leadership.com/book. This companion includes all journal questions and exercises from this book.

And go to ascendleadership.com/quiz to take our five-minute Impossible Freedom Quiz™, a quick way to identify your Middle Zone leadership style, biggest time and team leaks, and the next best step to reclaim your time, strengthen your team, and drive business growth without losing yourself in the process.

When you finish this book, you'll have everything you need to climb beyond the Middle Zone, lead with confidence and clarity, and build a business that fuels your personal freedom, not one that consumes it.

Welcome to the journey toward Impossible Freedom.

# YOU'RE STANDING AT A CROSSROADS: ARE YOU READY TO ASCEND?

Impossible Freedom isn't a luxury or an add-on. It's the solution. It's the cure for the urgent, silent crisis too many women leaders face today—a way to reclaim your time, energy, and joy without compromising your success. It's a proven path for how to grow a business that feeds you rather than consumes you. This book will show you how to shift from delaying what matters most to creating next-level business and financial growth that supports the life you deserve. It will empower you to close the gaps in your time and team so your actions, mindset, and vision finally align with your deepest priorities and values.

After our family trip to Mexico that I shared about earlier, I got some concerning results from a routine medical test called an A1C, which measures average blood sugar over the previous three months. My result was high enough to be considered prediabetic. I remember thinking: *Something has to change.* It was a wake-up call that pointed to a larger pattern. I had fallen into a pattern of putting off my health, convinced I'd focus on it when things calmed down or when I had more time. But time wasn't going to magically appear. I had to make different choices. Now, not someday.

So I did something so many leaders struggle to do: I asked for help. I hired a coach with expertise in what I needed. I got honest with myself not just about what wasn't working, but about what my most important priorities were. I began to shift my mindset and daily habits. I stopped waiting for permission to prioritize myself and started leading myself with care.

Since then, I've lost twenty-five pounds and feel more radiant than I have in years. I haven't reached some perfect finish line, but I'm on the path and no longer running in place, exhausted but not actually moving forward. I'm done postponing the life of Impossible Freedom I want to live. Because *someday* is how we stay stuck. Choosing to begin *now* is how everything changes.

Because without intervention, a reckoning always comes. Often it's a health scare, a fractured relationship, or a quiet but crushing moment of regret when you realize years have slipped by while you were too busy to truly live. That moment becomes the crossroads: You can rise to the call and choose a new way of leading yourself and your business, one that prioritizes your well-being as fiercely as your business goals, or you can stay trapped in the Middle Zone, treading water and risking everything you've spent years building.

You don't have to wait for a crisis or a reckoning to make meaningful changes, but if you wait too long, the costs will only compound. What starts as chronic stress can become serious illness, strained communication can turn into an irreparable rift, and what feels like a temporary sacrifice can turn into a lifetime of lost experiences you never get back.

So which path will you choose? This book is your invitation to rewrite the rules of success—and finally live the life your hard work was meant to make possible.

Let's get moving. There's no time to waste.

# THE FOUNDATIONS OF IMPOSSIBLE FREEDOM

## CHAPTER 1

# THE COST OF THE MIDDLE ZONE

*By Nadine and Derek Nicholson*

For us, nature isn't just a place—it's part of who we are and how we choose to live. We cherish, value, and prioritize our time outdoors and firmly believe in the positive impact that nature has on humans. One of our favorite pastimes is hiking in our own backyard, the Canadian Rocky Mountains. When our son, Keane, was seven years old, we headed out on our first springtime hike. He took off with excitement, leading the way with a bounce in his step, but as the trail grew steeper, his energy faded. His confidence dropped. Finally, Keane stopped and said, "I can't do this anymore. I need to stop."

We knew exactly how he felt. It was the first hike of the season, and our legs were also sore, but more than that, we recognized what was happening: Keane had hit the Middle Zone.

It happens in business too. You start with enthusiasm, fired up about a new idea or opportunity. You pour your heart, time, and energy into building something amazing. Then, one day, everything gets harder. Your head starts playing games with you, telling you it's impossible to go any further. You get scared, and your confidence crumbles. The joy and excitement that once fueled you disappears, and suddenly, staying where you are feels like the safest and only option.

But remaining in the Middle Zone isn't safe. It's where you get stuck, and staying there actually takes more effort than getting out. The real solution isn't to work harder or give up; it's to shift your focus, regain perspective, and move forward with renewed energy.

Instead of telling Keane to tough it out, we lightened things up and distracted him by asking about his favorite sports team. His face lit up as he talked about it, and without realizing, he started climbing in a different way. Every time his mind drifted back to how hard the hike felt, one of us pulled another question from our back pocket. Before long, we reached the mountain ridge. The view stretched out before us, and Keane beamed with pride.

That's what happens when you break free from the Middle Zone. You reach a new altitude where there's more room to breathe, see clearly, and move with confidence. Once you've experienced it, you'll never settle for staying stuck again.

In this chapter, we explore what the Middle Zone is in detail, how much it's costing you, and why the strategies that got you here won't take you further. We break down the hidden forces keeping you stuck: the Say/Do Gap™, where your time doesn't align with your true priorities, and the Support Gap™, where your team relies too heavily on you. We'll also explore the Time Leaks™ and Team Leaks™ that drain your energy and stall growth, along with three Middle Zone leadership types—Momentum Builder, Overworked Climber, and Exhausted Explorer—to help you identify where you stand and what's keeping you there. Lastly, we'll give you the secret to escaping the Middle Zone so you can finally feel fully lit up in business and life—*and* drive more financial growth at the same time: The Impossible Freedom Equation.

## WHAT IS THE MIDDLE ZONE OF SUCCESS?

Building a business is like climbing a mountain. It's challenging, exhilarating, and deeply fulfilling. As a high-achieving entrepreneur, you've already climbed higher than most. You put in the hard work. Pushed through obstacles. Hit the milestones. Earned the revenue. To the outside world, you look very impressive.

So why does it feel like you're working harder just to stay there? How do you break free without sacrificing all you've built?

This is the Middle Zone, a plateau where high-powered, high-achieving entrepreneurs, founders, and CEOs find themselves caught between the success they've built and the freedom they crave. At first, the Middle Zone doesn't seem like a problem. You've learned how to generate revenue, grow and scale your company, and master the art of pushing harder. But over time the weight of maintaining it all becomes exhausting. You're no longer running your business; you're trapped inside it. The flexibility and independence you once dreamed of now feel like a distant mirage, visible on the horizon but impossible to reach.

There are unmistakable signs that you've hit the Middle Zone. Your time isn't your own, you're weighed down by an overloaded calendar, you have too much on your shoulders, and stepping away (even for personal priorities) feels like a risk. You constantly have to hustle to the next thing. You're booked all day, often without breaks to eat or even pee, and you know it's not good for you. Strategic thinking seems out of reach because you have no extra energy to spare, as if every level up requires more effort than the one that came before. You keep telling yourself, "Once I hit \$________ revenue or get through the next quarter, things will get better." But they never do. Delegation and accountability feel stressful because your team leans on you for too much, and even when you try to off-load responsibilities, the weight of it all never fully lifts. You feel guilty taking a break and have a hard time relaxing because downtime isn't really downtime when the mental load never stops.

And the hardest part? You know something needs to change, but you don't know how to fix it without risking all you've built. Maybe it is a wake-up call like burnout, a missed family experience, an illness, a loved one's death, a creeping sense that your life is slipping through your fingers while you're buried in work. Or maybe it's just the quiet realization that this isn't sustainable. Despite understanding this fundamental truth, the Middle Zone still keeps you trapped, whispering the same false promise over and over: "Just push a little harder, and then things will get better."

They won't. Not with that strategy anyway.

## THE HIDDEN LEAKS THAT STEAL YOUR TIME, DRAIN YOUR ENERGY, AND STALL YOUR GROWTH

The way we learned to lead as high achievers is broken. Too many founders and CEOs trade their time, energy, and relationships for success—trapped in a cycle where sustained growth demands more from them, not less. They tell themselves they value freedom, family, health, and impact, but their calendars and team say otherwise. This disconnect creates two invisible forces that keep even the most successful business leaders stuck: the Say/Do Gap and the Support Gap.

At first glance, the problem at the core of these two gaps appears to be not having enough time. You're busy. Your calendar is full. You're juggling priorities, fighting fires, and trying to keep yourself and everything else afloat. But the real problem isn't how much time you have. It's the hidden leaks in how you use and lead your time. Unchecked, these leaks keep you stranded in reactive mode, forcing you to work harder just to maintain what you've already built. They drain your energy, stall your business growth, and pull you further from the freedom you once set out to create. But once you identify them, you can fix them.

**The Say/Do Gap:** This is the disconnect between what you say you value and how you actually spend your time. The Say/Do Gap shows up when your calendar is full of obligations but leaves no room for the people, priorities, and pursuits that give your work meaning. You say freedom matters, yet your schedule keeps you tethered to execution instead of vision. You say you want space to think, strategize, and rest—but your schedule keeps you trapped in day-to-day execution. You say your health is a priority, but your calendar last week shows zero hours on movement or doctor appointments. You say you want to be present with your family, but you worked through the weekend again. These Say/Do gaps fuel resentment, burnout, and time guilt. Closing Say/Do gaps is the first step toward Impossible Freedom.

The Say/Do Gap consists of three Time Leaks: time guilt, overworking, and overthinking. Even if you believe you're making progress in your business, these hidden Time Leaks keep you working longer hours while pulling you further from who and what matter most.

*Time Guilt:* This is the zero-sum struggle where you feel that you're missing out and can't win. You feel pulled in multiple directions and feel inner conflict about how you're spending your time no matter what you're doing. If you're working, you feel guilty for missing out on your personal life. If you step away from work, you worry your business will suffer, even though you know you need the break. Growth always seems to come at the expense of something else, making it impossible to be fully present where you are.

*Overworking:* This is the hidden trap of working harder to get ahead. You frequently work long hours but never feel like you're catching up or getting ahead. Stressors in your personal life may make it easy to throw yourself into business, where you feel competent and valued, but instead of having time to focus next-level thinking and making strategic moves, you spend most of your time in the daily grind, firefighting, handling last-minute issues, and reacting to problems that shouldn't be yours to solve. No matter how tightly you try to maintain control, you always feel like you're sliding toward being out of control. You worry that if you step back, everything you've built will fall apart and you'll lose the success you've built, and you often have little energy left for the people and things that matter deeply to you.

*Overthinking:* This is the mental energy leak. You second-guess decisions and often worry about what others will think, avoid difficult conversations, and overanalyze your choices trying to make the "right" choice, burning mental energy without making real progress. Decision fatigue keeps you stuck in a cycle of hesitation and uncertainty, leaving you exhausted instead of leading powerfully.

**The Support Gap:** This is when your team isn't yet operating at the level that truly frees you. It's the disconnect between having people in place and actually feeling supported by them. The Support Gap appears when delegation is inconsistent, roles are misaligned, or accountability keeps bouncing back to you. Even with strong talent, you still feel like you're holding everything together. It keeps you stuck managing instead of leading, and limits how far your business can grow. Closing the gap means building a team that moves mountains with you, not one that adds to your load.

The Support Gap consists of three Team Leaks: skill misalignment, fragmentation, and leadership leaks. No matter how hard you work, your business's growth will stall when you have a Support Gap.

*Skill Misalignment*: This is when you and your team spend too much time working outside of your strengths: what each person is best at, most passionate about, and what drives the most revenue growth. Instead, you struggle with inefficiencies, misaligned roles, skill gaps, and hiring challenges that stunt business growth and leave you, as the team leader, picking up the slack instead of focusing on strategic leadership.

*Fragmentation*: This is when you and your team struggle with cohesiveness and alignment. You work in isolation, communicate ineffectively, miss deadlines, waste time in indecision and inaction, overcomplicate simple things, and fall short of your best work. Collaboration is a challenge, and your overall efficiency is reduced.

*Leadership Leaks*: This is when you fear letting go of control, struggle with delegation and holding your team accountable without micromanaging. You avoid or delay making difficult decisions and have a hard time clearly communicating critical issues. Instead of having the time and space to mentor and lead your team, as well as the mental focus to work on next-level strategy, you get stuck between being too hands-on and too absent while creating unnecessary bottlenecks that slow down momentum.

The cost of ignoring the Say/Do Gap and Support Gap is significant, and it compounds over time. If you don't solve and close your Time and Team Leaks, you'll stay trapped in the Middle Zone—always working but never achieving the next level of business growth or the fulfilling personal life you deserve. Your business will remain dependent on you, and your own growth as an individual with ever-evolving career aspirations and goals will be hamstrung. Instead of scaling in a way that brings you freedom, you'll spend more and more time managing, maintaining, and treading water. Your personal life will continue to take the hit. No matter how much you say you value time off, health, and relationships, you'll always feel too busy to prioritize them. The longer you operate from within your gaps and let leaks drain you, the harder it becomes to shift into real CEO-level leadership.

## WHICH TYPE OF MIDDLE ZONE LEADER ARE YOU?

Not everyone experiences the Middle Zone the same way. Let's explore three types of leaders who find themselves stuck in the Middle Zone. Each leader faces different risks and requires different strategies to escape and drive business growth. We provide a real-life example of each leader, introducing you to three women whose journeys to Impossible Freedom we'll follow throughout the rest of this book (along with several others).

**Momentum Builder:** If you're a Momentum Builder, you're a high achiever making steady progress but facing inefficiencies that slow you down. You have a clear vision but struggle with subtle misalignments in time and team leadership, such as over-involvement in decisions, hesitancy to delegate, or unclear team roles. While you're on a clear path, these inefficiencies risk compounding over time, leading to slower growth, more stress, and unexpected obstacles. To move forward, you must refine your leadership approach and optimize your strategies before these leaks become major obstacles.

*Leader Example:* As the president of a defense technology company, Katie Bigelow had successfully led her organization through major growth in a traditionally male-dominated industry, but as the demands on her time continued to increase, she found herself at a crossroads. She was juggling both high-level strategic leadership and day-to-day operational management, and it was no longer sustainable. She knew she needed to make a change, but fear of making a mistake or disappointing others kept her paralyzed in the Middle Zone.

Katie was a Momentum Builder, a leader with a visible path forward, but internal resistance, overthinking, and uncertainty kept her from making decisions that would move her past the Middle Zone. She wasn't overwhelmed or burned out yet, but her leadership was not fully optimized. Without addressing the misalignments in her approach to team and time, she risked losing valuable momentum and business growth. In Chapter 5, you'll learn how Katie redefined what leadership looked like for her and grew her revenue without sacrificing her health, relationships, or joy.

**Overworked Climber:** If you're an Overworked Climber, you're gaining altitude, but it's getting harder to breathe. You're also experiencing growth but at the cost of your energy, decision-making clarity, and personal freedom. You're caught in a cycle of working long hours, constant problem-solving, and an overwhelming workload, which drains your ability to think strategically. Without intervention, you risk burnout, reactive decision-making, and becoming the bottleneck in your own business. Your next step is to identify and eliminate hidden workload burdens, such as decision fatigue and delegation resistance, so you can transition from survival mode to sustainable success.

*Leader Example:* For years, Stef Tschida built her business on the belief that relentless effort was the key to success. As the founder and CEO of Ripplea, an employee communications and change management firm serving Fortune 500 companies, she thrived on helping senior executives navigate rapid organizational change. But despite the steady growth of her company, Stef felt increasingly stressed, overloaded, and under strain despite the constant pressure to push even harder.

"I came from the corporate world myself and built my own business with the intention of having more of a life. As my own boss, I thought I had deprogrammed myself from my corporate hustle mindset, but I hadn't even scratched the surface," she recalled. "I was working long hours, convinced that success required constant effort. The reality? I was in my own way."

Stef was an Overworked Climber, an ambitious leader caught in survival mode, expending energy at an unsustainable rate. She was creating business growth but at the cost of her personal time, clarity, and sense of control. Like many in the Middle Zone, she faced a fundamental dilemma: continue pushing forward at the risk of burnout or take a step back and redefine success on her own terms. You'll learn across several of the coming chapters what happened when Stef escaped the Middle Zone.

**Exhausted Explorer:** If you're an Exhausted Explorer, you're deep in the Middle Zone, surrounded by trees with no clear view of the path below you or the summit above. You feel trapped in a cycle of exhaustion, constantly reacting to urgent demands and struggling to gain control of your time and vision. You often feel disconnected from your original goals, overwhelmed by decisions, and burdened by tasks you shouldn't be handling. And you worry about losing all the success you've built, yet staying where you are feels just as risky—maybe more so. If you continue on this path, overwhelm, resentment, and burnout will only get worse. To break free, you need to bravely press pause, take a strategic step back, reassess priorities, regain clarity, and restructure your leadership approach to prioritize decision-making, delegation, next-level strategy, and personal well-being over day-to-day firefighting.

*Leader Example:* For nearly two decades, Anne Staines poured everything into building Sagent, a social impact marketing firm dedicated to helping public agencies and purpose-driven organizations create meaningful change. The company grew under her leadership, landing major contracts and making a real difference in communities. But behind the success, Anne was exhausted. She had developed a strong leadership team, but she wasn't just leading—she was holding everything together. With extremely long workweeks, an unending stream of responsibilities, and a business that depended too much on her, she felt trapped. The dream of stepping back and enjoying the freedom she had worked so hard to create felt impossible.

"I was trying to cut down my work hours but was still being bombarded by the unexpected," Anne explained. "I had a long backlog of things I never had time to do, and full time for me had been sixty-, seventy-, even eighty-hour weeks."

Anne had reached a breaking point. She even considered a complete exit, walking away from the business entirely, to regain control of her life. That changed when we offered her a practical, achievable path to fundamentally shift her leadership approach so she could cut back her working hours while increasing her business revenue. You'll learn how Anne broke free from her cycle of overworked exhaustion to reclaim and own her time in Chapter 2.

Katie, Stef, and Anne—and the other founders and CEOs you'll meet throughout this book—were where you and other leaders are now. All three leader types share similarities, but each one experiences a different form of struggle in the Middle Zone. Momentum Builders need to fine-tune their approach, Overworked Climbers must shift from survival mode to sustainability, and Exhausted Explorers require a fundamental reset. Use the summary in Table 1 below to consider which type of leader you might be.

To find out for certain, visit ascendleadership.com/quiz and take the Impossible Freedom Quiz. In less than five minutes, it will reveal what type of Middle Zone leader you are, the hidden leaks in your time and team keeping you trapped by your business, and your best next step to regain control and scale with more freedom.

**Table 1.** Key Differences Between the Three Middle Zone Leaders.

| | Momentum Builder | Overworked Climber | Exhausted Explorer |
|---|---|---|---|
| **Current Situation** | Making progress but facing inefficiencies in time and team management. | Growing but struggling with long hours, constant firefighting, and decision fatigue. | Trapped in exhaustion, overwhelmed by daily demands, and disconnected from her vision. |
| **Main Challenge** | Small misalignments in leadership and delegation that slow momentum. | Working harder instead of smarter, leading to burnout and bottlenecking. | Reacting to urgent issues without strategic direction, causing frustration and loss of control. |
| **Risk of Staying Stuck** | Slower growth, leadership inefficiencies compounding into major obstacles. | Burnout, loss of clarity, stalled business growth due to unsustainable workload. | Deepening exhaustion, resentment, and inability to move forward effectively. |
| **Key Shift Needed** | Optimize time and team alignment to sustain momentum. | Eliminate hidden workload burdens and delegate strategically. | Step back, reassess priorities, and restructure leadership approach. |

## ESCAPE THE MIDDLE ZONE USING THE IMPOSSIBLE FREEDOM EQUATION

There comes a moment in business when pushing harder is no longer the answer. The strategies that got you here won't take you further (or higher), and the success you built is now costing you more than it's giving you. You're stuck in the Middle Zone, the high-stakes crossroads where you either elevate or erode.

Many entrepreneurs never escape. They burn out, plateau, or settle, believing that relentless effort is the only way forward. And the longer you stay trapped in it, the more it costs you—not just in time and energy, but in joy. In purpose. In the life you always envisioned for yourself. Deep down, you know it's time to break free, but if you try to push through using the same strategies that got you here, you'll only stay stuck, exhausting your energy without making real progress.

There is another, more sustainable, path.

The Impossible Freedom Equation is a proven leadership model designed to help you reclaim your time, unite your team, and remove you as the bottleneck, allowing you to achieve more financial growth without losing yourself in the process. It's the shift from being overloaded, reactive, and stuck to becoming decisive, empowered, and in control of your time. It's the transition from being the engine that drives your business to becoming the architect of a company that thrives without consuming you. Instead of pouring everything into work while your personal life waits on the sidelines, you build a business that fuels instead of drains the life you actually want to live.

This isn't just theory. The Impossible Freedom Equation is used by powerhouse leaders running seven- to nine-figure businesses to take back their time, energy, and life while scaling with more ease than ever before. When you apply it, the Say/Do Gap disappears, the Support Gap closes, and your business finally becomes a scalable, self-sustaining system. Because true leadership isn't about doing more; it's about structuring your business and life in a way that actually moves you forward.

Whether you're a Momentum Builder, Overworked Climber, or Exhausted Explorer, you're closer to achieving Impossible Freedom than you think because this reality isn't a fantasy or a luxury. It's a conscious choice. A leadership shift. A new way of thinking, structuring, and showing up in your business that rewires how you lead, live your best life, and drive business and financial growth. It starts with unlearning the lie that harder work is the answer. It starts with reclaiming your power—your time, your energy, your leadership.

It starts now.

You don't have to wait for someday to live the life you've always wanted. You can live a deeply fulfilling life that lights you up *while* driving next-business growth, without compromising one for the other. You can feel wildly accomplished and deeply at peace. You can give yourself permission (and recognize you have the right and the responsibility) to do what you want but think you can't. You can break free from the Middle Zone without losing an inch of your success.

And when you do? That's when the impossible becomes possible.

Now that you understand the hidden costs of the Middle Zone and the forces keeping you stuck, it's time to take action. In the rest of Part 1, we'll explore the two core Leadership Pillars of the Impossible Freedom Equation: Time Mastery (Chapter 2) and United Team (Chapter 3). You'll learn how to reclaim your time, close the Say/Do Gap, and align your calendar with what truly matters. Then we'll shift to the power of a strong team, including how to close the Support Gap, delegate effectively, and build a business that thrives without over-relying on you. From there, we'll dive into key Leadership Amplifiers: trusting your Wild Wisdom, making Brave Decisions, and having Courageous Conversations. By the end of this journey, you'll not only escape the Middle Zone, but also create a business and life designed for true freedom most founders and CEOs only dream of reaching.

# YOUR REFLECT TO RISE JOURNAL

**Mindset Shift:** The story of Keane's hike illustrates how shifting focus can help overcome obstacles. What mental shifts have helped you get through difficult moments in your business or career? What strategies could you try moving forward?

**The Cost of Staying Stuck:** What has staying in the Middle Zone already cost you, personally and professionally? What might it cost you if nothing changes in the next year?

**Breaking Free:** This chapter argues that staying in the Middle Zone ultimately takes more energy than learning how to break free. What emotions come up when you think about leaving the Middle Zone behind? What fears, hopes, or doubts surface when you imagine stepping into the next level of growth in your business and life?

**Middle Zone Leaders:** Which Middle Zone leader type (Momentum Builder, Overworked Climber, or Exhausted Explorer) relates most to you right now? What signs or patterns from your business or life led you to this conclusion?

**Taking Action:** If you could change *one* thing this week to start shifting out of the Middle Zone, what would it be? What small step can you take today?

**Community Connection:** What insights from this chapter do you think would benefit other entrepreneurs or business leaders in your network? How could you start a conversation with them about the Middle Zone and what it takes to break free?

Get the free book companion with all
reflection questions and exercises at
ascendleadership.com/book.

## CHAPTER 2

# TIME MASTERY: THE FOUNDATION OF FREEDOM

*By Nadine Nicholson*

B efore I founded and grew Ascend Leadership Co. to what it is today, I had a successful, demanding career in corporate communications. I led a team of more than a hundred corporate communications professionals, earned international recognition, advised top executives in North America, and managed multimillion-dollar business operations. As a high performer, I got where I was through a single-minded, unshakeable belief that hard work was the path to success. This belief drove me to work myself to the bone because, quite frankly, I didn't know any other way. My success in business was tied tightly to my sense of identity. Without one, I wouldn't have had the other.

In my mid-thirties, at the height of my corporate career, Derek and I married and soon began trying to have a baby.

Getting pregnant was a struggle for us. But after enduring a long, arduous path, our son Keane became our precious miracle. The moment I held him, a wave of gratitude and awe crashed over me; I had never known love like this. I took a year of maternity leave, then jumped right back into the thick of my career and soon earned a big promotion. My responsibilities increased massively.

When Keane was eighteen months old, I was working seventy hours a week and rarely saw him for more than half an hour each day. We had hired a live-in nanny from the Philippines who took care of him while Derek and I worked full-time. On some level, I knew how I was living wasn't right for me, but I couldn't envision how to change it. At that same time, my dad died three weeks after being diagnosed with cancer. His passing was life-altering for me. Something fundamental shifted in how I understood my world.

*What am I doing?* I asked myself. *Why did I even have a child if this is how I'm going to live?*

I could finally see clearly. The beautiful baby boy we had worked so hard to bring into this world was on the back burner in my own life. I was compromising my relationship with him for business growth. I was also compromising my relationship with Derek, my health and well-being, and all the parts of my life outside work that brought me joy. While I didn't wake up every day "trying" to be in a Say/Do Gap, my dad's sudden passing was the wake-up call I needed to see that I was blindly operating from a societal belief that personal sacrifice was the price of success. Something had to change—radically.

In Chapter 1, we introduced you to the Say/Do Gap and its three Time Leaks. This chapter explores Time Mastery, a core Leadership Pillar of the Impossible Freedom Equation, as a powerful antidote to the chronic time scarcity that plagues high-achieving leaders. You'll learn how cultural conditioning and inherited beliefs fuel the Time Myth, a deceptive narrative that convinces us we have all the time in the world, yet never enough time for what truly matters. Through personal stories, client transformations, and practical frameworks, this chapter breaks down the six elements of Time Mastery and shows how closing your Say/Do Gap leads to more alignment, fulfillment, and business revenue. By the end, you'll not only see time differently, but also know how to begin reclaiming and leading it on your path to Impossible Freedom, where you'll be living a fully lit-up life *and* driving more financial growth at the same time.

## THE TIME MYTH YOU DON'T KNOW HAS SHAPED YOUR LIFE

How we think about money is always a hot topic in the business world, but you know what too often flies under the radar? The lessons we learn and internalize about time that shape our entire lives. Your story may be similar to ours: Derek and I both grew up watching our fathers overwork, sacrificing time with family and their own well-being to make ends meet. Financial struggles are undeniably real, important, and require prioritizing, but it's the underlying moral principle I want to highlight that is problematic: the idea that compromising yourself is somehow noble, a belief that's often paired with the mistaken notion that there's no other choice.

We live in a hustle society. One that glorifies busyness, equates worth with productivity, and leaves little room for rest, rejuvenation, and reflection. We are not taught to value our time or our lives. In fact, the opposite. We are repeatedly, relentlessly taught that it's selfish to protect our time and value it above all else. Want your bank account to grow? Applause and backslaps. Want to reserve space in your calendar for yourself? Eyebrows raised. Our worth is tied to how much time we sacrifice in pursuit of work, money, and status. This is where the Time Myth takes hold.

The Time Myth is a powerful, invisible trap that tricks you into believing two opposing lies at the same time: that you have all the time in the world and "someday" will always be there waiting for you, and that you never have enough time for what really matters. In both cases, the only solution that seems viable is to keep sacrificing. These lies and illusions keep you stuck, always pushing what's most important to you farther down the road while convincing you that once you get through this next season, this next project, this next deadline, something will change. Then you'll finally be able to focus on everything you've kept on the back burner for so long. But that moment never comes.

You wake up months, years, even decades later, wondering where all that supposed "someday" time went. And the hard truth? You were right; the time was lost. Time is your most precious, nonrenewable resource, and you won't get it back. The real tragedy isn't just the lost time itself, but what it cost you: the relationships, the self-respect and self-worth, the adventures, the creative projects, the experiences that would have made you feel lit up and truly alive. It's easy to look back and see the trade-offs, but when you're in the middle of it, the Time Myth is so pervasive, so deeply ingrained in how we operate as a culture, that you don't even realize you're making trade-offs.

I recognized the impact that the Time Myth was having on my life in a moment of radical clarity after my dad died. Although I'd reached the pinnacle of achievement in my corporate career, I felt like a personal failure. I was sacrificing everything truly important to me, and suddenly it didn't make any logical sense. My life was defined by time scarcity rather than time abundance. I wasn't spending my short, finite time on this earth wisely at all. I'd become a victim to time, constantly spread too thin, constantly living in an energy of depletion and fear, constantly rushing, pushing, hustling, worrying, exhausting. I knew in my heart that I had to put my well-being and relationships at the center of my calendar. The gap was so painful that if I kept going in the same direction, I'd live to regret it deeply (more than I already did).

The misbelief that sacrificing your time is noble, and that you have both all the time in the world and no time right now, is why very few people truly master the leadership of their time. It means going against the grain in a way that makes you, and often those around you, uncomfortable. It means living by your own time frames rather than someone else's. It means challenging the belief that you have to keep grinding, that you have to keep proving yourself, that you aren't good enough if you don't work as much as possible, that one day there will be a perfect moment to finally prioritize what matters.

Do you ever catch yourself saying, "I'll do that someday"? Maybe it's that dream trip, time with your family, prioritizing your health, starting a new business, or finally starting the creative pursuit you've been talking about for years. You know it's important, yet someday keeps slipping further away. The truth is that someday is a trap. The more you push things off, the further you get from living the life you actually want. As you learned in Chapter 1, this is the Say/Do Gap: the space between what you say matters most and what you actually do with your time. If you say your health, family, joy, and freedom are priorities, but your calendar tells a different story, filled with obligations that pull you in all directions, you have a Say/Do Gap that will never close itself, and that gap creates stress, guilt, resentment, and regret because, deep down, you know you're not living in alignment with what you truly want.

So how do you make a change? How do you escape the Middle Zone? How do you forge a path to Impossible Freedom? You build Time Mastery into the very foundation of your business and life.

## WHAT IS TIME MASTERY?

Time Mastery is one of the two core Leadership Pillars of the Impossible Freedom Equation. It's the practice of structuring and designing your time and energy with radical intention so your schedule reflects your core values and highest-impact priorities, not just your urgent demands, so you stay lit up, renewed, and prioritized. It's about reclaiming, owning, and leading your time, rather than allowing external pressures, obligations, and societal conditioning to dictate how you use it. Instead of living from the outside in, you live from the inside out, placing *you* at the center of your calendar. Time Mastery is a state of being, not a state of doing, and it's achieved one intentional, brave decision at a time, creating incisive, intentional action that focuses on progress over perfection and alignment rather than accomplishment. Because the more you live in alignment, the more accomplishment flows to you in both business and life.

Let's explore six key elements of Time Mastery.

1. **Eradicating the Say/Do Gap:** Mastering time requires identifying and closing the gaps between what you *say* matters and what you actually *do* with your time so your decisions and actions reflect and fulfill your true priorities.

This means no longer pushing off your well-being, relationships, personal growth, and creative projects in favor of an endless cycle of single-minded work that neglects everything else in your life. It means eliminating the Time Leaks of time guilt, overworking, and overthinking.

2. **Defying "Can't"**: Many founders and CEOs operate under self-imposed or socially conditioned limitations and obligations about how they *should* use their time. Time Mastery involves identifying and eliminating these false "can'ts" that keep you trapped in an outdated model of success. By challenging these limiting beliefs, you open the door to new possibilities and a more fulfilling, impactful relationship with time, your business, and yourself.

3. **Designing an Entrepreneurial Time Rhythm:** For high-achieving leaders, Time Mastery isn't just about better scheduling or time blocking. It's about strategically designing a weekly and monthly time rhythm that supports both professional success and personal fulfillment, without forcing trade-offs between the two. You know you've found the right rhythm for you when your work and life don't compete with each other but rather feed each other's growth. It's not about balancing two opposing forces. It's about integrating them in a way that energizes both. The shift from a zero-sum mindset ("If I spend time on myself, my business will suffer") to a yes/and approach ("When I invest in myself, my business benefits too") is a game changer. It's one of the most effective ways to solve time guilt. Designing your rhythm includes identifying energy-draining distractions, prioritizing tasks that align with your Natural Genius (the intersection of your strengths, passions, and revenue-driving activities), and building a structure that sustains both your business

ambitions and your personal well-being. Done right, your time becomes a source of power, not pressure.

4. **Shifting from Time Management to Time Leadership:** Traditional time management focuses on efficiency or getting more done in less time. Time Mastery goes beyond this to help you cultivate time leadership, which prioritizes actively designing your calendar in a way that creates more time rather than less. Instead of managing your time, you reclaim and *lead* it by putting what lights you up and makes you feel most alive at the very center of your schedule, then protecting it with fierce integrity. This means setting clear boundaries, saying no to distractions, and staying true to your needs, even if it means disappointing others.

5. **Expanding Time Through Presence:** A key realization in Time Mastery is that time slows and expands when we are fully present. Many high achievers struggle with presence, feeling guilty when they aren't working and distracted when they are with loved ones. This creates a cycle of time guilt—never feeling like you are where you should be while also establishing a fearful belief that you should be further ahead in your business, career, and personal life by now. By learning to fully ground yourself and engage in the present, time stops feeling like a scarce resource and instead becomes something that feels abundant.

6. **Intentional Design—Structuring Time for Maximum Freedom:** Mastering time isn't just about mindset (although mindset is important). Mastering time also requires deliberate action. This includes reverse-engineering time off (starting with the breaks, vacations, and personal time you want to protect and then building your calendar around them), alongside setting up sustainable work rhythms, designing business structures that support freedom,

and ensuring that what energizes and fulfills you is no longer displaced to the edges of your life. Intentional design and maximizing freedom diminish drivers of negative self-talk, procrastination, and energetic drains while simultaneously increasing spaciousness, confidence, self-respect, and self-worth.

When I saw in my own life what I now call the Time Myth and Say/Do Gap, I realized I was living with a mind-boggling amount of time guilt. Stepping away from work to focus on my family made me worry about falling behind at work. While working at my desk, I missed my son. While with Keane, my mind drifted to unanswered emails. When answering emails, I wondered when I'd finally get to exercise, escape my desk to get outside, or eat something healthy. No matter what I did, I felt like I should be somewhere else, doing something else, more productive, more valuable. That's time guilt. It's a zero-sum game you can never win.

On top of my time guilt, years of overworking had worn me down. I'd been in overwork mode long before I gave birth to Keane. I was so focused on what I thought I needed to achieve that I never questioned why I was working really hard, and when my personal life felt difficult, my work became the one space where I felt competent, validated, and in control. I threw myself into my professional life, trying to keep all the plates spinning, giving everything of myself until I wasn't sure what was left. I couldn't breathe, but I also couldn't stop. I didn't realize it at the time, but overworking allowed me to avoid confronting the deeper truth: I wasn't living my life the way I wanted to.

Underneath it all? Overthinking. Quiet, constant, exhausted overthinking. I questioned whether I was a good enough mom, I overanalyzed decisions, second-guessed myself, and avoided the real conversations I needed to have, especially with myself. I was burning mental energy on every little choice because I didn't have the clarity or confidence to fully trust my inner wisdom. I was stuck. Always moving but never getting anywhere that felt good.

Then my dad died, and I finally understood deep in my inner knowing that Keane didn't only need a mom who brought home a big paycheck. He needed a happy, rested, nourished mom who was present in her own joy, career, and motherhood. At this turning point in my life, I knew I had to give myself permission to redesign my time with intention and in alignment with the values I wanted to live by, not the values that had trapped me in what no longer served me. I didn't want to work as much as I was, and I didn't want to be a full-time stay-at-home mom either. There had to be a happy, meaningful middle where I could find freedom and work-life harmony.

When I told my boss about my plan to resign, she gave me an insight that will stay with me forever. "During the last ten years of my career, I've lost five years of my life from stress," she said with vulnerability.

In my mind's eyes, a metaphorical chocolate brown Venetian blind came down in front of me, blocking my view of her. My inner wisdom was sending me a message, trying to tell me: *Don't let this happen to you.* I was already being groomed to be her successor, but I didn't want that role. I felt certain it was time to move on. My boss's honesty taught me invaluable lessons about Time Mastery:

1. Vulnerability creates truth.
2. Life gives us inner wisdom when we are present.

3. Her experience didn't have to be my experience; I could create my own.
4. The years I'd lose to stress were far more important than staying in my job.
5. I didn't know exactly what I'd do next for work, but I knew it would be related to what I was already doing, and I'd get to build it from scratch myself.

I'm grateful to her. She gave me the gift of a truth I needed to hear that helped me confidently leap into freedom. Importantly, working in corporate wasn't the problem. Time Leaks were my problem. I was drowning in time guilt, over-working to prove something I didn't even believe in anymore, and giving all my energy to overthinking rather than making bold, aligned decisions from my inner compass. I was letting time slip through my fingers. When I accepted what was deeply misaligned in my life, I could finally take control, close my Say/Do Gap, and begin redesigning how I used my time.

## HOW FOUNDERS AND CEOS ELIMINATE THEIR TIME LEAKS

Today I'm privileged to help powerhouse, high-achieving leaders close their own Say/Do Gaps to escape the Middle Zone and ascend to Impossible Freedom. To help you see how this process can work in your personal and professional life, let's explore real examples of how some of our clients have eliminated their Time Leaks.

**From Time Guilt to Reclaiming Fifteen Work Weeks and Doubling Revenue:** Stef of Ripplea was the picture of business and financial success, but behind the scenes, she'd gotten herself stuck in a cycle of overwork and time guilt. Stef was trapped in hustle patterns: long hours, reactive decisions, and relentless urgency. The Say/Do Gap was real for her and getting bigger by the day. She valued freedom and strategy in theory, yet her calendar told a different story.

"The pace, the grind, the workload, the hours—it all felt very unsustainable," Stef explained. At the same time, Derek and I could see how she held a lot of skepticism that making radical change was possible. "This idea of working differently, living differently, having more ease and joy and spaciousness, *and* making more money? It's so counter to everything I've been programmed to believe."

Despite this skepticism, Stef borrowed our belief what seemed impossible was actually possible and hired us as her executive leadership coaches. We began dismantling her belief that success requires suffering. She rebuilt her schedule around high-impact work, reclaimed over six hundred hours per year (or fifteen workweeks), and let go of exhausting busywork. Stef's story is a powerful example of how Time Mastery, including strategic decisions, aligned scheduling, and courageous boundaries, can transform a high-achieving leader stuck in the Middle Zone into a confident, focused leader driving business growth from a place of alignment, not exhaustion.

**From Overworking to Owning her Time:** Anne of Sagent spent twenty-five years building a business that made a real difference, but behind the social impact-driven work was a heavy cost. She was working up to eighty hours a week and constantly firefighting as her team's go-to problem-solver. The responsibilities were endless. Anne reached a point where she felt like throwing in the towel and exiting the company, despite knowing deep down she didn't want to.

"All I knew is I couldn't keep going like that," she recalled.

Anne wasn't new to leadership development. She had worked with business coaches and participated in CEO round-tables. But the changes never seemed to stick. As the company continued to grow, she still ended up filling many of the gaps. Sagent still revolved around her, and the idea of real freedom felt out of reach.

Then Anne met me and Derek, and she discovered a different way forward. We guided her to challenge societal thinking and find her inner truth. Rather than trying to work smarter within the same system, she needed to redefine the system entirely. After meeting with her leadership team to share the vision for her elevated CEO role at Sagent, her team members were excited to help Anne succeed and work fewer hours. They quickly agreed to do all they could to transition even more work from Anne and build a business that could continue to grow while Anne maintained oversight without getting bogged down in day-to-day operations.

Letting go was uncomfortable. Anne had to reset expectations, especially with herself. But the results were undeniable. By eliminating unnecessary tasks, focusing on work that made the biggest difference, and creating space for personal time without guilt, Anne reduced her working hours by 75 percent. She's no longer a pinch point in the company. Anne says her leadership team has been a huge reason the company is doing even better than ever, with even more potential for growth because growth is not limited by the amount of time she can physically give it.

Anne's now in her business two days a week, three weeks per month, and takes the fourth week off. After spending years trapped and exhausted in the Middle Zone, she now has more energy and freedom to enjoy her life.

While many of Anne's competitors were laying people off and even closing their doors, Sagent had its most profitable year ever, with Anne working fewer hours than ever before.

"I used to believe," Anne said, "that working less meant sacrificing business stability and growth. I really wanted to achieve the vision that Ascend Leadership Co. helped me create. Now I see that stepping back has actually propelled my company forward. I can also see that I still had doubts that my new vision was possible, so I had to suspend my disbelief and be willing to let go of my former way of seeing my role. I'm proud to say I'm functioning for the first time in the history of the company as a true CEO. Sagent is healthy and no longer a day-to-day worry for me."

**From Overthinking to Leading with Clarity and Alignment:** As president of Ramar Foods, a third-generation family business, Susie Quesada carried the weight of legacy, leadership, and team well-being on her shoulders. Her calendar was packed, she and her team were burning out, and every big decision seemed to come with a spiral of overthinking. Despite her deep belief in self-leadership, Susie found herself hesitating on tough decisions, replaying scenarios in her mind, fearing missteps, and second-guessing what she knew in her gut to be true.

"I needed to pause and reassess how I really wanted to lead moving forward," Susie realized. That's when a focus on Time Mastery became her turning point. Working with us at Ascend Leadership Co., Susie began to recognize the Say/Do Gap in her leadership—saying she valued sustainability and balance but modeling stress and indecision, especially because personal and professional lines often blur in family-run businesses. To eliminate the Time Leaks of overthinking and overworking, she restructured her leadership team, set clearer boundaries, and created space for strategic decision-making and personal well-being.

Today Susie leads with clarity and alignment rather than constant mental churn. Her team is stronger, her schedule is more spacious, her revenue is higher, her relationships are stronger, and the legacy she's building is grounded in intention rather than stress. Her story illustrates how Time Mastery isn't just about getting more done; it's about thinking less, deciding faster, and creating aligned purpose.

## THE RADICAL OUTCOME OF TIME MASTERY

Time is your most precious, nonrenewable resource. Mastering how to reclaim, own, and lead your time is one of the most powerful leadership skills you can develop in today's hustle society. At its core, Time Mastery helps you shift from being reactive to being proactive. It challenges the deeply held belief that sacrificing time is noble and necessary for success and instead encourages an unapologetic approach to structuring time around your values, true desires, and Natural Genius.

Your Natural Genius is the unique intersection of your strengths, passions, and revenue-driving activities, including the work that energizes you, aligns with your purpose, and creates meaningful impact. It's the state of being and action where your skills feel natural, your contribution is highest, and your time yields the greatest return. Operating from your Natural Genius allows you to lead with clarity and ease, rather than burnout and overextension.

This shift also means leaving behind the Time Myth, the illusion that you simultaneously have all the time in the world and no time at all to focus on what matters most. It asks you to stop making trade-offs that postpone the life you want in exchange for more hustle and, instead, nurture and protect your time with fierce integrity. Because you *can* create harmony between your business and life while bringing in revenue in a more joyful, easeful, and aligned way. No more time guilt, inner conflict, and energy-draining distractions. Time scarcity becomes time abundance.

What's it like to truly master your time? Everything changes for the better. Your energy increases. Your creativity flourishes. You listen deeper, have more authentic conversations, and connect to your spirituality. You become more focused, rested, and grounded in the present. Your financial success grows not because you're working more, but because time now reflects your Natural Genius. You stop waiting for "someday" and start living now. Time Mastery isn't about squeezing more into your schedule or micromanaging your minutes. It's about stepping into leadership over your life and business so every moment reflects what truly matters to you. It means operating at a higher altitude where there's room for more life—more joy, presence, and fulfillment. And it requires three things: decisiveness, integrity, and courage. Decisiveness to realize that "someday" is a trap. Integrity to align your time with what you truly value. And courage to stay true to yourself, even if it means disappointing others.

If you want a business that thrives without costing you your life, if you want to lead without being held back by false "can'ts," and if you want to be truly present for all of life's adventures, you have to radically rethink your relationship with time. Time is the ultimate equalizer. It's the global currency we all share, the common value and basis for our economy. We all have the same amount of time each day. Other than birth, death, and basic biological needs, nothing unites humankind and the human experience quite like time. Despite this shared currency, or maybe because of it, time is a mystery. It can't be touched or felt. It's elusive, enigmatic, and, in a way, unsettling. We never know when our time will run out, so we must treat the time we do have as the freedom, opportunity, and gift it is.

## HOW TO ACHIEVE TIME MASTERY: STEP-BY-STEP

The first step to achieve Time Mastery is identifying and closing your Say/Do Gap, the space between what you say matters and what your calendar actually reflects. This is where time guilt, overworking, and overthinking quietly drain your energy, keep you stuck in the Middle Zone, and erode your freedom. When you close the Say/Do Gap, you'll start to experience a new level of clarity, alignment, and momentum. Here's how to begin.

**Say/Do Gap Eradicator:** Start here. Use this five-step process to uncover what's really going on beneath your busy schedule and begin making aligned decisions today.

### Step 1: The Say/Do Gap

- What is your "say"? What do you say you deeply want to be, do, or have?
- What's your current "do"? What are your actual actions and choices?
- What values are not being honored by how you currently spend your time?

### Step 2: Your True Desire

- If you were truly honoring those values, what would you be doing differently?
- Who would you become by choosing these more aligned choices?
- Why is this important to you? What's your real reason for changing this?

### Step 3: The Can'ts

- What fears or stories are telling you that you can't be, do, or have what you say you want? (In Chapter 8, we'll help you uncover more "can'ts" and show you how to transform them.)
- Why does this feel like too much, too soon, or too hard?

### Step 4: Inner Compass

- What does your inner compass, instinct, and knowing say about those fears and can'ts? (In Chapter 4, you'll learn this is your Wild Wisdom.)
- How are those fears and can'ts not true?

### Step 5: Choose

- What actions and choices will you choose now? What brave, inspired action will you take this week?
- On a scale of one to ten, how committed are you to actually following through on that action and why?
- What would make that number a ten in terms of commitment?

- What will you do when you catch yourself wavering or falling back into old habits?

These questions, answered in order, can bring clarity to your current reality and help you begin the internal shift required for sustainable change, but clarity alone won't get you there. You need to follow it up with bold, external action.

**Three Radical Actions to Build Time Mastery:** Once you've identified your Say/Do Gap and what truly matters, you're ready to begin making space for the life and business you actually want. Derek and I designed the following three radical actions to help you do just that, quickly and powerfully.

1. Identify the 20 percent of activities that drive 80 percent of your company's revenue. Make those your focus. Prioritize the highest-impact work (i.e., your Natural Genius work) and let go of everything that doesn't generate meaningful results or align with your purpose.
2. Eliminate, automate, or delegate everything that drains your energy or falls outside your Natural Genius. Time Mastery doesn't mean doing more. It means doing less of what's not in your Natural Genius. Protect your energy by removing or off-loading tasks that keep you stuck in the weeds.
3. Schedule at least three hours of CEO time per week. Create space for strategic thinking, visioning, and leading instead of reacting. If you're always in motion but never moving forward, CEO time is how you rise above the noise and take the long view.

The cycle of time guilt, overworking, and overthinking ends here. You don't need to do more to feel like you're enough.

You can't earn Impossible Freedom through exhaustion. And you don't need to wait for "someday" to start living by your own values and definition of success. You *can* decide when you want to work, how you want to work, whom you want to work with, and how much money you want to earn. The freedom you're craving isn't in some nebulous future. It's in the choices you make today. It's time to start living like you mean it. It's time to learn how to feel fully lit up in business and life—*and* drive more financial growth at the same time. We're here to show you how.

# YOUR REFLECT TO RISE JOURNAL

**Time Myth:** This chapter introduces the Time Myth, the misbelief that you have both all the time in the world *and* no time for what really matters. Where do you notice this illusion showing up in your life and business? How has it influenced your choices?

**Time Leaks:** Which of the three Time Leaks (time guilt, overworking, and overthinking) do you relate to most right now? How is it impacting your energy, calendar, or relationships? Which of the real-life founder and CEO examples described in this chapter do you see yourself reflected in?

**Say/Do Gap:** Where is there a noticeable gap between what you say matters to you and what you actually do with your time? What would your calendar look like if it fully reflected your values?

**Redefining Success:** This chapter challenges the long-held societal belief that business success can only come through personal sacrifice. If you were to let go of this belief, what would change? What does success look like when it includes freedom, joy, spaciousness, and ease?

**Taking Action:** Which of the three radical actions (identifying and focusing on your Natural Genius work, eliminating what drains you, and scheduling CEO time) feels most urgent for you? What's one decision you can make this week to start reclaiming your time?

**Community Connection:** What parts of this chapter would spark meaningful conversations with other entrepreneurs, founders, CEOs, or other leaders in your life? Is someone you know stuck in the Time Myth? How could you invite them into a new way of thinking about time?

## CHAPTER 3

# UNITED TEAM: SUPPORT THAT MOVES MOUNTAINS

*By Derek Nicholson*

For most of my life, I believed I had to do everything on my own. That belief drove me. At times, it even protected me. But eventually, I learned that the very thing I thought was keeping me safe was holding me back.

My dad worked in oil and gas, and much of his job revolved around entertaining clients. In the 1970s and 1980s, that practice meant long nights out eating and drinking, sometimes not coming home at all. I remember one Christmas Eve when he didn't show up until very late. No call, no warning. Just a drunk entrance into a tense and worried household on what was supposed to be a magical night. My parents fought often and loudly. As a kid, I lived in fear, not just of the yelling, but of what might happen if my mom decided she'd had enough.

She didn't work outside the home, and I knew she couldn't afford to provide for me and my sister on her own.

So I decided to take care of myself, to be the mature, stable one who could always be counted on. And that's exactly what happened. My hard work paid the way through university, leading to a business degree and early leadership roles in corporate sales and business development. By twenty-three, I'd bought my first house. By all accounts, I was successful and prided myself on being self-sufficient. I didn't need help or ask for support. Everything was under control. Beneath it all lay the belief that kept me going: *Depend only on myself.*

Years later, I became a dad.

The day after our son was born, Nadine turned to me and asked, "Do you feel love for him?"

"I don't even know him yet," I admitted. That moment of detachment shook me. I'd spent so many years focused on myself—on performance, on control, on independence—that I didn't know how to connect with my newborn son right away. Not only was I responsible for someone else, but for my own son, a little human who depended on me and Nadine completely. A deep sense of commitment and protection rose in me, unfamiliar but undeniable. As a result, everything I'd done to survive, everything that had made me successful, suddenly felt incomplete. I felt extremely unprepared.

One night, not long after Keane was born, Nadine went swimming, and I stayed home alone with him. He screamed for hours with intestinal gas. I tried everything. Nothing worked. By the time he finally fell asleep on my chest, I was shattered. When Nadine walked through the door, she took one look at me and asked, "What happened?" She could still see my terror.

I told her the truth. That I felt helpless. That I didn't know what to do. That I wasn't sure I could do this. She didn't judge me. She offered to call Deb, her postpartum doula, who calmly reassured me that I was doing just fine. Deb showed me a few techniques and normalized what I was feeling, and in that moment, I experienced something I hadn't felt in a long time: relief. Relief that I wasn't alone. Relief that I didn't have to figure it all out by myself. Relief that I could trust more than just myself.

That moment cracked something open in me, and it planted a seed of knowing that I didn't yet have the words for: Support doesn't make you weaker; it makes you stronger.

A year later, Nadine and I enrolled in a training program for professional coaches that I mentioned earlier in the Preface of this book. Watching that room of strangers share openly with each other many vulnerable things about their lives felt foreign to me. I realized, however, that they were united in their common cause, while I felt nervous and awkward.

*Is this how people are supposed to relate to each other?* I wondered. *Is this how I'm supposed to relate to other people?*

Growing up, my sister called me cold and unfeeling. Sitting in that room, watching people connect on a level I had never experienced, I got it. I realized just how detached I had become. I wasn't lacking relationships. I was lacking depth. Trust. Connection. Support. In that training, I discovered what it meant to truly be supported not just professionally, but personally. I started to soften. To open. I stopped trying to do it all alone and started letting people in. That's when everything changed.

Two decades later, I now coach and mentor founders and CEOs who are overwhelmed, over-functioning, and often convinced that if they want it done right, they have to do it themselves. Sometimes they try to get help from their team but don't feel like they can get team members to rise up or deliver in a way that's valuable to them as the owner. I help them see that they already have a team; it just might not be united yet. I help them shift from managing helpers to mentoring leaders. From surviving the daily chaos to creating systems of trust and support. From holding everything together by force to letting themselves be held.

Because the truth is your business was never meant to run on your back alone. You can only escape the Middle Zone and ascend to Impossible Freedom when you have the right people beside you.

That's my "why." My dad was a slave to his work and clients. Our family paid the price. Now I guide founders and CEOs like you to break that cycle, to build a business that runs without compromising your relationships, health, or sanity. I guide you to become an empowered leader who thrives rather than suffocates on your own success and who experiences the kind of Impossible Freedom that's only possible when you're no longer going it alone. You don't have to wait another day, and you don't have to earn rest or deserve support. You already do.

In this chapter, we'll explore what it truly means to lead with support, not just effort. You'll learn why a United Team is essential for sustainable growth and how to shift from over-functioning to empowering yourself and others. We'll look at the key leadership habits that create trust and cohesion, break down the three Team Leaks that quietly erode your momentum, and walk step-by-step through how to develop and nurture a team that doesn't just follow your lead but amplifies it. By the end of the chapter, you'll fully understand that your team is larger and more powerful than you think. You'll learn that support isn't a luxury; it's the strategy for living your best life and driving business growth, without the trade-offs keeping you trapped in the Middle Zone. Because your next level of freedom isn't about doing more; it's about doing differently.

## WHY YOU NEED A UNITED TEAM

I hear common myths about leading teams all the time:

"More people equals more work."

"I can't let go of control of the operations."

"I just need to work harder to get ahead."

These myths are symptoms of the Middle Zone. Too many leaders find themselves at a painful crossroads: They've built something great, but now it's running them. The business that's supposed to give them freedom demands, instead, every ounce of energy and attention they have. The to-do list is endless. The decisions never stop. And even when growth is happening, it's hard to enjoy the momentum because the moment things start moving faster, fear creeps in. You have a list of questions running on a loop in your head: *Can my team handle this? Can I step away and unplug? What if it all falls apart? What if things get too far behind?*

This is where the second Leadership Pillar of the Impossible Freedom Equation comes in. A United Team is a high-performing team and support system that drives your vision forward so you're free to lead strategically, not manage reactively. Having a United Team isn't a luxury for when you reach a certain level of success; it's a prerequisite for sustainable business growth and personal freedom at every stage of your journey. When your team is truly united, you no longer have to carry the weight of your business alone. You can step back without losing control. You can trust others to lead within their Natural Genius. And you can stop holding your breath every time growth begins to accelerate.

You, like many leaders, deny yourself this kind of team because you equate more people with more problems. You fear becoming the manager of a team that still depends on you for every answer. Or, worse, you overwork to avoid overburdening others, leading to a cycle of exhaustion, martyrdom, and isolation. What you may not realize is that the problem isn't that you have a team or a big enough team. The problem is that you don't have a United Team, and you're not leading it with intention.

A United Team goes beyond job titles or organization charts. It includes the people you pay and the people you don't: your employees, contractors, mentors, clients, colleagues, and referral partners, as well as your life partner, parents, relatives, friends, and more. These are the people who believe in your vision and stand behind your leadership. They're not just checking boxes; they're actively contributing to your success. And, just as importantly, they trust you enough to lean in and let you lean back.

After I'd worked years for corporate medical technology companies, selling products and services into the government-led healthcare system, I decided to leave corporate and work inside the healthcare system. I led five multidisciplinary home care teams in a system where clinical managers were almost always doctors or nurses. With a business degree and no clinical medical training, I faced skepticism right away. But instead of trying to convince them or prove myself, I focused on what I knew: how to create strong teams and empower people. I made it clear I wasn't there to tell them how to do their jobs. They were the experts. My role was to foster conditions where they could thrive, which meant shifting decisions closer to the front lines and trusting their judgment.

At first the people in my teams were competitive, guarded, and unsure of one another. In our meetings, I told them, "You don't have to be friends, but you do have to respect each other." That became a turning point. Over time they stopped acting like rivals and started acting cohesively. And it showed. We avoided unnecessary conflict, stayed within budget, and always had shift coverage. Our team culture was so strong, people began sending me résumés without even seeing a job posting. The medical professionals who had doubted me and my leadership model became my biggest champions.

Without a United Team like this, founders and CEOs are forced to operate with an invisible Support Gap and Team Leaks that quietly drain their time, energy, and confidence. These include skill misalignment (people working outside their strengths), fragmentation (disconnected communication and siloed efforts), and leadership leaks (difficulty delegating, mentoring, and staying focused on the big picture). We'll discuss these more later in this chapter, but for now, what's crucial to know is they create drag, like biking uphill with a flat tire. You're working harder than you need to, and every gain feels fragile.

But when your team is united, everything shifts into a higher level of being. Roles are aligned with your people's strengths. Communication becomes fluid. Trust is mutual. You stop micromanaging and start mentoring and inspiring. You stop hiring helpers and start developing leaders. You delegate not because you're overwhelmed, but because it's smart. The result? You free up your time for higher-impact work, and you do it without guilt or fear.

Some of the most profound lessons I've learned about building United Teams came not from traditional hierarchies, but from environments where authority was informal and influence had to be earned. In one of my consulting contracts with an operational excellence network in the oil and gas sector, I worked with engineers who were expected to lead their peers without being their formal supervisors. These were smart, capable people, but many struggled with the idea that leadership isn't granted by title. It's developed through trust. My job was to help them find that trust, to become the kinds of leaders others choose to follow.

One moment stands out vividly. After sitting in on a highly technical meeting, one of the engineers asked me what I'd heard. I laughed and said, "Honestly? It sounded like blah blah science, blah blah big word."

He grinned and said, "That's exactly what I hear when you talk about leadership."

That exchange, humorous as it was, revealed something deeper. We each brought a kind of expertise the other lacked and valued. That mutual respect became a foundation of the work. In United Teams, it's not about everyone knowing the same things; it's about recognizing and respecting what each person brings to the table.

Think of it like riding a bike downhill. When your team's foundation is solid and everything's flowing, momentum accelerates quickly, but if you don't trust the bike to hold together, you'll hit the brakes. That's what so many leaders do. They instinctively, subconsciously slow down at the very moment their business is gaining momentum because they don't believe their team, or the infrastructure, can keep up. A United Team is the bike that *does* hold together. It's what allows you to keep going, to go faster, and to enjoy the ride.

The bottom line is this: a United Team is not just a business tactic. It's a freedom enabler. It's the difference between surviving growth and soaring through it. It's how you expand your impact, increase your joy, and finally create a business that supports your life, not the other way around. But to build that kind of team, you have to start in the right place—not with your people but with yourself. Because what looks like a team problem is almost always a leadership problem.

## SOLVE YOUR LEADERSHIP PROBLEM TO SOLVE YOUR TEAM PROBLEM

I've spent much of my professional life learning what makes a team work and what quietly, often invisibly, tears it apart. At Ascend Leadership Co., I've worked with founders and CEOs across industries, and the patterns repeat: disengagement, misalignment, confusion, and miscommunication. What I've learned is that these aren't employee problems. They're leadership problems.

When I meet a leader struggling with performance, burnout, or morale, the first thing I do is look past the numbers and ask, *What does leadership look like here? How are people being set up, or not set up, for success?* Too often workplace culture has been allowed to form by accident. Norms are assumed. Values are stated but not lived. Expectations are implied, not agreed upon. Delegation is treated like a to-do list instead of a conversation. These are not minor issues. These are foundational cracks in the structure of a team.

Take employee engagement, for example. In some companies, only 10 to 20 percent of employees report feeling engaged, and the overall percentage of engaged employees in the US is only 31 percent.[1] That number should make any leader stop in their tracks. What if that number were 80 percent? What would those companies be capable of then? Many people's first instinct is to point to the workforce—people just don't care anymore, young people don't want to work, the wrong people were hired. I don't buy that. I've hired so-called "problematic" millennials and watched them flourish, not because they changed,

---

[1] Jim Harter, "U.S. Employee Engagement Sinks to 10-Year Low," Gallup, January 14, 2025, https://www.gallup.com/workplace/654911/employee-engagement-sinks-year-low.aspx.

but because the leadership around them did. I took the time to recruit intentionally, to train, to communicate expectations, to show appreciation, and to mentor. The results were undeniable.

Leadership is not about doing everything yourself or being the smartest person in the room. It's about enabling others to thrive. That means letting go of control while still being deeply invested in outcomes. Too many leaders confuse being responsible for a result with being the one who does everything. But here's the thing: As your business and revenue increase, your individual capacity to manage every outcome declines. You can only manage the process, and the process is people. If you lead them well, if you unite them around your shared vision, the outcomes follow.

Delegation is one of the most misunderstood aspects of leadership. When leaders delegate, they often just off-load tasks. "Do this," they say, and then wonder why it doesn't get done the way they want. True delegation is about giving someone ownership and agency, not chores. You set the vision, define what success looks like, ensure they have the skills and support, and then trust them to figure out how to get there. That doesn't mean you disappear on them; it means you become a guide, a safety net, and a resource.

And if a mistake happens? Great. That's a learning opportunity, not a failure. People need space to experiment, reflect, and improve. In science, this principle is essential: Scientists intentionally stress and even break systems to expose weaknesses and improve designs. Before a space shuttle ever launches, teams put it through extreme testing, pushing every part to the limit and forcing failures, so they can identify flaws, fix them, and ensure the mission's success. This process doesn't signal incompetence; it's the hallmark of excellence. Similarly, in leadership, if mistakes are punished, a culture of fear takes root, but if they're framed as critical steps toward mastery, a culture of growth and resilience flourishes.

On one of the youth baseball teams I coached, we had a kid who joined us as a second baseman. He had all the technical skills—he could catch, throw, and hit—so he filled the role on paper. But what made him invaluable wasn't listed on any stats sheet. He was the team's comic relief. When the pressure was high and the team was tense, he had a natural ability to lighten the mood, crack a joke, and bring everyone back down to earth. We encouraged that part of him, gave him permission to be that kind of leader on the bench, and it changed everything in key moments. People bring more to a team than just their job title or skill set. When you recognize and make space for the full range of what someone offers, that's when a team truly starts to perform at its highest level.

I saw this again while coaching a hockey team that had a true Cinderella season. In sports, this describes an underdog team's unexpected success. We only lost one game all year. Not because we had the most skilled players or the best talent on the ice, but because we were united in every way. The players trusted each other, supported one another, and played as a team. That unity was our secret weapon.

One specific example stands out. We had just won our third game in a tournament to advance to the final. One of our players, Tyler, scored a hat trick (three goals) to propel us to that win. The team chose him as player of the game, and when he received the award, this fourteen-year-old boy stood in front of his teammates and said, "I could not have done any of that without you guys creating the space and getting the puck to me in the right place and at the right time."

It was one of the most memorable leadership moments I've witnessed—because it was a moment of pure humility. Tyler didn't just celebrate his own performance; he elevated the team that made it possible. That's a high-level leadership competency we don't talk about enough. Humility isn't about downplaying your strengths, but rather about recognizing that success is rarely a solo act. In that short speech, Tyler demonstrated something many adults still struggle to embody: the ability to own his contribution while giving credit to others. Moments like that are what make a team truly united. They remind us that leadership isn't just about standing out; it's about standing together.

In contrast to these moments of team unity, leadership, and character revealed through levity and humility, I witnessed a very different dynamic while coaching another youth baseball team. When we made an unexpected comeback to tie the score late in a game, the opposing team's coach called his entire team to the pitcher's mound and singled out one of his players, blaming him for a mistake. It was an attempt at public accountability, but it came at the cost of the player's confidence and the team's cohesion. They lost the game. This example is a powerful reminder that shame, even when it's masked as feedback, erodes team unity. Whether someone is ten years old or a tenured executive, the ability to thrive in a team hinges on feeling safe, supported, and respected.

At a large North American oil and gas company, I worked with a cross-departmental team that was struggling with this same challenge. These were professionals from different business units, tasked with standardizing process across the company. They had to communicate with each other but knew very little about each other. Initially, there was competition and turf-protecting: *Who's the expert? Who's the top performer? Whose site or department does the best?* To shift that dynamic, I guided them to do something simple but transformative. We developed a "team résumé." Each member documented their full range of skills, projects, passions, aspirations, and experiences—not just what their title said. We discovered hidden capabilities, new sources of insight, and more importantly, a new respect for each other. People started to see the team as more than the sum of its individual parts. That trust allowed for better collaboration and innovation, a stronger sense of shared purpose and values, better outcomes, and getting the right people on the right tasks.

None of that would have succeeded without establishing clear team norms. Norms are the operating system of a team. They are how we communicate, how we make decisions, how we hold each other accountable. Too often these norms are assumed, not articulated. Whether I'm working with kids on sports teams or adults in offices, the process is the same. We sit down, name what matters—like punctuality, respect, and responsiveness—and decide as a group what we're willing to commit to. We talk through what each norm means in real terms. We define how we'll handle it if someone doesn't uphold it. We ensure accountability. Even something as small as a jar for late arrivals, where people drop in a dollar for team lunch, sends a message: We're in this together.

I didn't come out of business school knowing how to lead people. Business school taught me finance, strategy, and operations. It didn't teach me human beings. The real leadership education came later through hands-on experience (including mistakes), mentorship, coaching, and a lot of self-reflection. One of the best places to start? Look in the mirror. Ask yourself: *How do I like to be led? What motivates me?* For me, Dan Pink's model of motivation—autonomy, mastery, and purpose—resonates deeply with me.[2] I want autonomy, mastery,

---

[2] Daniel H. Pink, *Drive: The Surprising Truth About What Motivates Us* (Riverhead Books, 2009).

and purpose in my own work, and I believe most other people do too. We all want to feel that our work matters, that we're great at it, and that we have some control over how we do it. If you structure your leadership approach around those three simple things, you'll see your team transform.

And transformation doesn't require perfection. I've worked with entrepreneurs, CEOs, new managers, and seasoned executives. The ones who grow are the ones who are willing to be honest, to try, to let go of ego, and to invest the time to learn. Leadership isn't a talent; it's a practice. And like any practice, it gets stronger with repetition, reflection, and the right kind of support. Similarly, a United Team isn't an accident. It's a result of intentional leadership. When you provide space for people to step into their strengths, when you make values visible and norms explicit, when you delegate not just work but ownership and agency, you stop managing tasks and you start leading people. That's when the magic happens. That's when you start driving next-level business and financial growth without having to make personal trade-offs that trap you in the Middle Zone.

## CLOSING THE TEAM LEAKS THAT STOP YOU AND YOUR BUSINESS FROM EVOLVING

Leading a truly United Team goes far beyond organizational charts or casual team-building activities. It requires leaders to consistently invest their time, energy, and resources into cultivating a cohesive, high-functioning team. Too often team-building is reduced to surface-level activities ("Let's go bowling and become friends"), but camaraderie alone doesn't create alignment. A United Team is built through deliberate, ongoing leadership. It means engaging in meaningful conversations about shared values, cultural norms, collective goals, and what success looks like together. It means co-creating explicit agreements about how team members will collaborate and communicate. This level of intentionality doesn't happen by accident; it takes daily commitment. Strong teams aren't born. They're built—one conversation, one agreement, one decision at a time.

When alignment, trust, and cohesion are missing from your team, you have a critical Support Gap that needs closing. In Chapter 1, we introduced you to the three Team Leaks that make up the Support Gap: skill misalignment, fragmentation, and leadership leaks. I've seen them in our clients' businesses across industries, in corporate environments, and in sports teams I've coached. They're universal, and they're costly. Here we're going to dig deeper into each leak so you know how to spot them in your own work and leadership. Because once you do, you'll never look at your team the same way again.

Let me start with skill misalignment. This one's common and often invisible until it's already doing damage. It happens when people are in the wrong roles, working outside their natural strengths and areas of expertise (their Natural Genius), or don't have the experience or support needed to thrive. What I see most often is that many leaders rely too heavily on job titles or original hiring decisions, rather than taking the time to explore someone's full skill set. They forget that people bring more than what's written on their résumé and end up leaving so much potential on the table.

You need to move beyond job titles and start asking, "What does this person actually bring to the table? What else can they contribute?" When you do that, you not only maximize the value of each person, but also eliminate a lot of the competition and internal jockeying that happens when people feel boxed in. People stop feeling pitted against each other for advancement and instead feel united around the real goal: the success of the team and business.

Fragmentation is the second Team Leak. It's what happens when communication breaks down, deadlines get missed, and no one is quite sure who's doing what. Everyone's operating in their own silo, often overcomplicating things that should be simple. It's a sure sign that there's a misalignment somewhere upstream, either in structure, expectations, or leadership clarity.

The third type of Team Leak, leadership leaks, is often the hardest to admit. I've lived it myself, and I've coached leaders through it. These leaks happen when you avoid tough conversations, when you micromanage because you're too burned out to mentor, when you bottle up issues instead of addressing them head-on with Courageous Conversations, or when you become a bottleneck because you're taking on too much instead of trusting your team and delegating effectively. Leaders who want to empower their teams without micromanaging often feel stuck, like they're walking a tightrope between over-involvement and abdication.

I worked with a client named Susie who started with this leadership leak. You met her in Chapter 2. She runs a successful business with three hundred employees, and when I met her, she was deeply concerned about her team's burnout. What she didn't realize until we worked together was that she was modeling burnout herself. She cared so much about her team that she was sacrificing her own well-being, and that was sending a message to everyone else: *This is what leadership looks like.* Nadine and I helped her see that she was her number one asset, and investing in elevating her own leadership wasn't indulgent; it was essential for both herself and her team.

Another client, Laura, came to us as a powerhouse ghostwriter who was trying to shift into more of a leadership role in her business. A ghostwriter is a professional writer who creates content, such as books, speeches, and articles, that are officially credited to another person. She was tired. She was overwhelmed. And she was carrying the belief that only she could do the work at the level her clients expected. She wanted to delegate, but she didn't fully trust that her team could deliver the same quality, or that clients would accept it if she wasn't directly involved.

Together we uncovered that Laura had outgrown the "doing" role in her business. Ghostwriting had once been her Natural Genius, but now it had become a zone of excellence: something she was still great at but no longer energized by. Worse, it was holding her back from stepping into the leadership role her business, team, and clients truly needed her to fill. She was operating outside of her business's growth needs, hanging onto too many tasks, and blocking the path for others to step up. Over time she surrounded herself with a United Team that she could truly trust, hired a project manager, and let go of the idea that the quality of her business's work and the client experience would diminish if she didn't do everything herself. That shift allowed her to scale her impact while creating more personal freedom.

These stories aren't unique. They're reflective of what so many leaders experience, especially women leaders. There's guilt. There's doubt. There's the belief that being emotional makes you weak, or that being liked is more important than being respected. I've watched leaders struggle to have Courageous Conversations with team members, not because they don't know what needs to be said, but because they're worried about how it will land. And yet the ability to communicate clearly, kindly, and directly is one of the most powerful tools a leader can have. Courageous Conversations are at the heart of a United Team. To have them, you need to be grounded in what we call Wild Wisdom, or your inner knowing. You need to make Brave Decisions that align with your values. And you need to trust that having Courageous Conversations with honesty and empathy will strengthen your relationships, not harm them. We'll explore each of these Leadership Amplifiers in Part 2.

A United Team isn't built overnight, and it's not about getting it right every day. When your Team Leaks are sealed, something powerful happens: Your people's roles align with their strengths, your team's efforts mirror your vision, and what's said matches what's done. It takes work. It takes clarity. And above all, it takes courage. But when it clicks? When you step into your full role as a leader, when you let go of what no longer serves you, and when you finally have the right support system? That's when your business becomes not only successful, but also sustainable and scalable to new heights. That's when you become not just effective but free.

## HOW TO BUILD YOUR UNITED TEAM

The idea of building a United Team might sound big, abstract, or overwhelming, especially if you're already maxed out. But here's the truth: Creating this kind of support system doesn't require an HR overhaul or a massive hiring spree. It begins with something far simpler and more powerful: awareness. You already have a team. The question is—are they united?

A United Team isn't just about having more people. It's about having the right people in the right roles doing the right work, which fosters a culture of trust, alignment, and shared vision.

It's about giving yourself permission to stop doing it all alone and start prioritizing a business that supports you back. Here's how to begin.

**The United Team Builder:** Start here. Use this five-step process to start creating the kind of aligned, empowered support that helps you live your best life and drive business growth, no trade-offs required.

## Step 1: Assess Your Current Support System

Before you can strengthen your team, you need to know what you're working with. This means taking inventory of your current support system, both in business and in life. Start by asking yourself:

- Who is currently helping me (paid and unpaid)?
- Who else could be helping me but isn't yet?
- Where do I consistently feel overburdened, stretched thin, or unsupported?

This includes obvious team members like your employees or contractors but also less obvious members. For example, you don't hire or pay your partner, a client or former client, or even a friend who calls from time to time. Recognize that support comes in many forms—emotional, logistical, strategic— and it all matters. Often we're surrounded by more people ready to offer support than we realize. We just haven't been intentional about activating or aligning them. Many people also don't ask others to support them because they say, "I don't want to be a burden to them."

## Step 2: Identify Your Highest Value and Best Use of Time

Once you know who's in your corner, the next step is figuring out what only you can do and what can be handed off. This is one of the hardest mindset shifts for high achievers to make, especially if you're used to being the fixer, the finisher, or the one who holds it all together. But time is your most valuable resource, and not every task deserves it. Ask yourself:

- What are the things that only I can do in this business?
- What are the tasks that drain me, distract me, or take me away from high-impact work?
- What would I gladly never do again if I had the right person in place?

Your goal here is to identify the work that energizes you today—not when you founded your business—drives results, and aligns with your long-term vision. Then, as hard as it may be, commit to delegating everything else and eliminating what really doesn't need to be done.

## Step 3: Fill Key Roles with Leaders, Not Just Helpers

A common trap many entrepreneurs fall into is hiring people who can help rather than people who can lead. Helpers wait for instructions. Leaders solve problems. Helpers create more work for you. Leaders remove it.

When you're building your United Team, you want people who think critically, act decisively, and take ownership of outcomes. This doesn't mean hiring only C-suite executives.

It means finding individuals, at any level, who are empowered, engaged, and invested in your mission. Look for:

- People who ask, "What's the goal?" not just "What's the task?"
- Individuals who take initiative and anticipate needs.
- Teammates who are energized by outcomes, not micromanagement.

The shift here is from delegation to empowerment. You're not handing off work. You're nurturing capability and confidence in others.

## Step 4: Create Rhythms of Trust and Accountability

A team won't unite on its own. Trust and alignment are fostered through consistent, intentional interactions. That's why the most effective teams operate on shared rhythms and cadences that create clarity, connection, and accountability. This might include:

- Weekly or biweekly check-ins with your core team.
- Values-aligned hiring practices that reinforce your culture.
- Clear role definitions so no one's stepping on toes or working in isolation.
- Collaborative problem-solving where voices are heard and ideas are shared.

Trust doesn't come from big, dramatic moments. It's earned in the small, steady moments. It's earned by showing up consistently, keeping your word, and creating space for others to do the same.

## Step 5: Anchor in Support During Growth Moments

Here's one of the most important lessons I've learned: It's when things start going well that your support system matters most. When momentum kicks in, your natural instinct might be to hit the brakes. That fear of dropping the ball or losing control of the bike creeps in, but that's exactly when you need to trust your team and lean into the systems you've implemented. Don't give in to self-sabotage. Instead of slowing yourself down, trust the bike will hold as the hill gets steeper. With a United Team in place, you can keep going. You can grow, scale, and even enjoy the process because you're not doing it alone. So, in these moments of acceleration:

- Pause and remind yourself of who's supporting you.
- Communicate clearly about what's needed as things ramp up.
- Ask for help, early and often.

Momentum is not the time to retreat. It's the time to *rely*.

**Your Turn—United Team Activation:** If you're ready to put this into action, here's a simple but powerful exercise to kick-start your United Team journey. Grab a pen and journal your way through the following:

1. List your current team. Capture everyone contributing to your success, both paid and unpaid, inside and outside your business. For example, this may include your employees, clients, vendors, colleagues, family, friends, mentors, financial advisor, doctor, nutritionist, house cleaner, personal trainer—anyone who supports you in being your best self. Think expansively.

2. Where are your Support Gaps? What roles, relationships, or responsibilities need shoring up?
3. What's one conversation or decision you've been avoiding? Maybe it's asking for more help. Maybe it's finally delegating something. Maybe it's letting someone go. Choose one action that will move you closer to a United Team and take it.

Founders and CEOs often forget that health, home, and relationships are part of what sustains their ability to lead. At Ascend Leadership Co., our clients light up when they finally realize that a United Team includes calling in that support system. Not because a leader is failing, but because they're human. No one is meant to do this on their own. Building a United Team starts with one clear step: deciding you don't have to do it all alone. You are no longer a solo climber or a lone achiever. You are an expedition leader and empowered guide. This shift is the key to everything that comes next because once you stop believing strength and leadership mean doing it all yourself, you open the door to a level of momentum and support that can move mountains. You begin to forge a team where people rise to meet the challenge alongside you. Where trust is earned and extended. Where delegation becomes ownership and agency, and leadership becomes shared.

Your business doesn't only need hands and helpers. It needs hearts and minds aligned with your vision, ready to walk beside you. This is what a United Team makes possible. You'll finally be able to step back and breathe, and you'll finally be able to move forward faster, with less friction and more joy. So take that first step. Make the list. Close the gap. Have the conversation. Rally your team. Because the moment you choose to lead with intention and clarity, you stop carrying your business and start being carried by it. A United Team doesn't just help; it liberates.

# YOUR REFLECT TO RISE JOURNAL

**Leadership Myth:** This chapter challenges the belief that needing support is a sign of weakness. Reflect on where you learned your ideas about independence and leadership. How have those beliefs and experiences shaped how you lead your team or resist being supported?

**Team Leaks:** Which of the three Team Leaks (skill misalignment, fragmentation, and leadership leaks) do you see most in your current team or support system? How are they showing up in your business and life right now, and what impact are they having on your time, energy, or confidence?

**Intentional Leadership:** This chapter emphasizes that a United Team doesn't form by accident; it's the result of intentional leadership. In what ways have you been leading reactively instead of intentionally? What would it look like to lead your team with purpose, clarity, and design instead of by default?

**Taking Action:** What's one conversation, decision, or act of delegation you've been avoiding that would move you closer to having your own United Team? What action will you take this week to reduce your Support Gap?

**Community Connection:** Who in your life might benefit from the idea that their team is bigger than they think? How could you start a conversation with them about shared leadership, building support, or designing a business that doesn't rely on one person alone?

Get the free book companion with all
reflection questions and exercises at
ascendleadership.com/book.

# LEADERSHIP AMPLIFIERS

## CHAPTER 4

# WILD WISDOM: YOUR INNER COMPASS

*By Nadine Nicholson*

I n Part 1 we introduced you to the foundations of Impossible Freedom. We explored the Middle Zone, a plateau where high-powered, high-achieving entrepreneurs, founders, and CEOs—especially women—find themselves caught between the success they've built and the freedom they crave. We exposed the Say/Do Gap and Support Gap as key barriers, the draining effects of Time Leaks and Team Leaks, and leadership types, pitfalls, and common experiences that reveal how constantly trying to work harder and do more can instead stall your personal and business growth. Through the lens of the Impossible Freedom Equation, we began to reframe what's possible, showing you how its two core Leadership Pillars, Time Mastery and United Team, are not luxuries but necessities. By demonstrating the shift from endless hustle to intentional alignment, and from solo climber to exhibition leader, Part 1 laid the groundwork for you to escape the Middle Zone and then start to feel more lit up

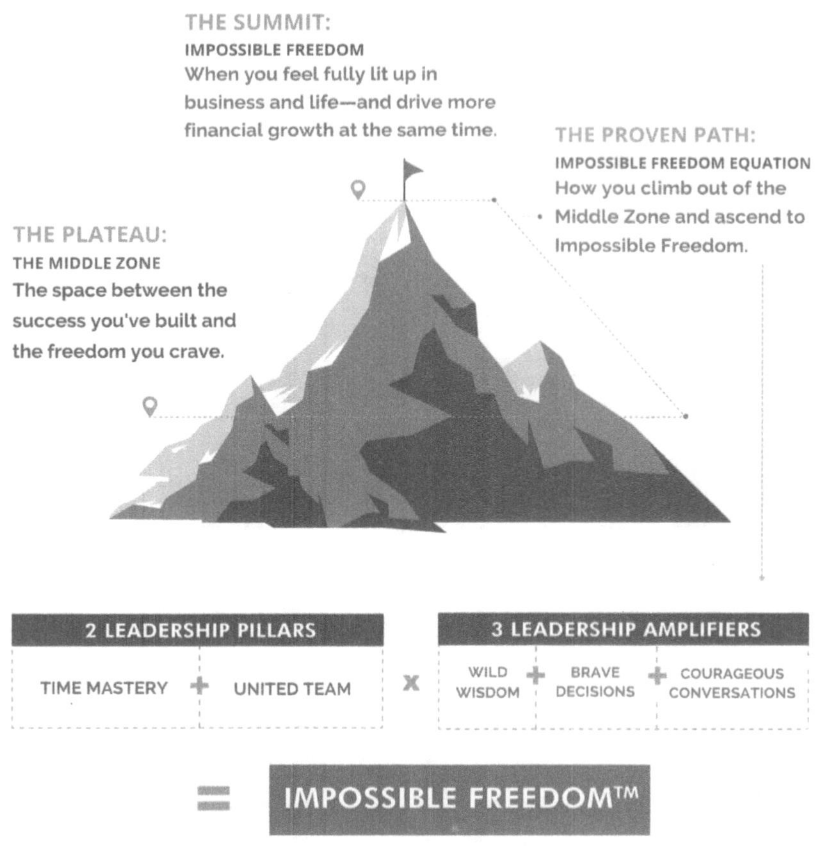


**Figure 1.** The Impossible Freedom Equation.

in your business and life *while* driving more financial growth in your business. We're repeating Figure 1. The Impossible Freedom Equation here to remind you about how the equation works.

Now that the foundations are in place, Part 2 invites you to step fully into your power. This is where the journey toward Impossible Freedom accelerates. With your time and team unlocked and abundant, you're ready to activate the three Leadership Amplifiers: Wild Wisdom, Brave Decisions, and Courageous Conversations. Together they form a decision-making cycle: Wild Wisdom helps you access your inner clarity and intuition, often through nature and embodied practices, grounding you in self-trust and inner truth. That clarity then supports Brave Decisions: bold choices made without analysis paralysis or fear of external judgment. These decisions, in turn, lead to Courageous Conversations, where clear, honest, values-aligned communication shifts your personal and client relationships, supports your team, and expands your impact. As you move through this cycle again and again, the Leadership Amplifiers don't only support Time Mastery and United Team—they elevate them. They make the Impossible Freedom Equation fully operational, helping you lead with more clarity, conviction, and ease.

In this chapter we begin with Wild Wisdom, the key to transforming your inner compass into a powerful tool for leadership and business strategy. Derek and I have learned that every leader finds their way to this clarity differently. What matters isn't where you access your inner knowing. It's that you learn to trust it completely. You'll discover how to reconnect with your heart and gut and why the inner knowing that exists below your shoulders must come first on the path to Impossible Freedom. We'll explore how nature serves as a powerful shortcut to clarity, how fear often blocks access to your deepest truths, and how embodied practices can shift you from confusion to confidence and conviction. Through client breakthroughs, practical tools, and lived experiences, you'll discover how to lead not by pushing harder, but by tuning in more deeply. Whether you're navigating uncertainty or seeking alignment, this chapter will help you stop chasing answers and start listening to the wisdom that's already within you.

# TRUSTING YOURSELF IN THE WILDERNESS OF LEADERSHIP

When I was fifty years old, I hiked one of the most beautiful places in the world: the Alpine Circuit high above Lake O'Hara, British Columbia. I climbed the mountains and gazed out at the turquoise waters of the stunning alpine lake. Lake O'Hara represents untouched nature. One of the most sought-after and cherished backcountry outings in Canada, it is lovingly and strictly protected by the federal government; only a handful of people are granted access to the area each day.

Remote. Wild. Precious.

Every moment I looked around, there was so much beauty. I felt in awe and thought to myself, *I feel so alive and lit up!*

I felt that way because I was in an environment that reminds me of things that matter deeply to me, including being intentional about how I spend my time by taking radical responsibility for my calendar and my life so I'm walking my talk by doing what I say matters to me. Abundance and possibility surrounded me; I felt fully connected with myself in nature. I remembered the importance of being unapologetic about my life, my truth, and what I value most—and to never stop the powerful work of growing, exploring, and challenging myself.

The hike made me feel . . . at home. Peaceful. Inspired. Grateful. Wild and wise.

When was the last time you felt this way?

There's a truth you already know but may have forgotten. Beneath the hustle, beneath the pressure to perform, beneath the constant mental calculation of the million tasks, obligations, and decisions demanding your attention, your deep, inner wisdom has always been with you. Derek and I call this your Wild Wisdom. It's the part of you that already knows the answers, even when your brain is spinning in circles. This wisdom lives in your body, your breath, your heart, and your gut. It becomes accessible the moment you stop overthinking and start trusting yourself, tapping into your connection to nature (the natural world) and what should be second nature to you (what feels most instinctive and true). When everything feels like it's out of control, reconnecting with your Wild Wisdom is the first step to finding the path forward.

Wild Wisdom is not a metaphor. It's a leadership and business strategy rooted in nature, spirit, and real-world practice. It's about becoming deeply attuned to your inner compass so you can lead with unwavering clarity instead of fear, uncertainty, confusion, or a need for external validation. For many of our clients, accessing Wild Wisdom means taking a deliberate pause away from the noise of daily business demands and into a more instinctual way of being.

Most entrepreneurs and leaders are programmed to use only the 20 percent of wisdom that lives above their shoulders, where the analytical mind resides. But that leaves out the 80 percent of wisdom that lives in the rest of their body, below their shoulders. Our heart and gut are biologically wired to process complex information and to give us signals about what's right, wrong, aligned, or off course. The problem is that we're often too busy, or too overwhelmed, to hear what those signals are saying. Leaders get stuck in overanalysis, decision fatigue, or fear-based thinking because they ignore their most important support and guide. They second-guess themselves. They avoid decisions they already know need to be made. They say yes to things they don't want. And over time they lose touch with their natural instincts.

The remedy? Nature.

# NATURE IS THE SHORTCUT
# TO YOUR WILD WISDOM

If Wild Wisdom is the destination, nature is the most direct and fastest path to reach it. Nature exists in two deeply interconnected dimensions: the outer world, what we often call the Great Outdoors or Mother Nature, and our inner world, the unique rhythm and truth of our individual nature. Both offer essential distance from the forces that pull us away from ourselves: the relentless pace of information, the weight of external expectations, the confinement of office walls, the noise of obligations and opinions. In their place, nature offers stillness, spaciousness, and a return to what is most real and enduring within us.

External nature encompasses both outdoor spaces where we can directly engage our senses and natural environments that help us process challenges and insights. These physical surroundings ground and restore us. Internal nature, on the other hand, is our authentic self, shaped by our unique needs, interests, experiences, and values. This internal landscape can be accessed through personalized practices that act as gateways to our inner knowing, such as meditation, prayer, yoga, spiritual verse reading, and breathing exercises.

The fastest way to harmonize these two dimensions is through Mother Nature. We often encourage our clients to close their eyes, breathe deeply, and feel their feet on the ground. This simple embodiment practice moves their focus away from their fear-projecting brain and into their wisdom-holding body and spirit. When you immerse yourself in natural settings while honoring your internal rhythms, Wild Wisdom begins to emerge. Each person's internal nature is unique, but Mother Nature serves as a universal shortcut to accessing it. Rather than forcing solutions at a desk, bringing your challenges outdoors allows your internal nature to help process and resolve them. The key is to shift from actively working on a problem to allowing nature to work on it, creating space for intuitive insights and deeper understanding.

But in today's age of information and technology overload, our connection to Wild Wisdom is easily and often disrupted. Constant digital stimulation floods our senses, especially through fragmented visual input, keeping our minds in a near-perpetual state of over-activation. An endless stream of data enters through our screens, overstimulating the brain and dulling the body's natural signals. This creates a mental environment that is primed for anxiety. We're pulled into our heads, caught in loops of overanalysis, worry about the past, and catastrophizing about the future. Our nervous systems become habituated to alertness, leaving little room for calm, embodied presence.

In this state, the deeper signals of our inner knowing (the instincts, emotions, and intuitive nudges that live below the shoulders) are drowned out by noise. We begin to rely solely on external metrics and validation to make decisions, outsourcing clarity to whatever scrolls across our feed. Over time our internal compass fades. The very faculties that once helped us survive, adapt, and thrive as a species become inaccessible. Wild Wisdom, by contrast, roots us in the present moment. It quiets the mental noise, restores our connection to what's true and essential, and helps us lead from clarity rather than anxiety.

That's why nature should not be an "escape" from the office and your busy work schedule. It should be an integrated, strategic part of your work and leadership. Getting outdoors—truly outdoors, away from your phone, meetings, and artificial lighting—changes your biology. It lowers your heart rate and blood pressure, reduces cortisol, and restores the body's natural rhythms. The shift is not only psychological, but also physiological. The higher oxygen concentration in a forest, the lapping of waves along a shoreline or boardwalk, the rhythmic movement of walking, or the visual patterns of your natural environment of choice all contribute to calming and regulating your central nervous system. It also helps activate both hemispheres of your brain for creative problem-solving. The more time you spend in nature, the more your body remembers: *This is how I'm meant to feel.*

Beyond the biological reset, nature creates something equally powerful: spaciousness. It creates space for thoughts to settle, insights to surface, and truths to emerge. Nature strips away the "shoulds," "can'ts," and distractions. When you're in the forest, on the trail, or by the water, you're no longer performing, reaching, or controlling. You're simply being. And from that place, you can hear your truth again and see the path forward. Through this process, you begin to bypass societal conditioning, tap into your instinctual knowing, and access a deeper, unfiltered understanding of yourself and your business challenges. This connection to Wild Wisdom becomes the foundation for making Brave Decisions and leading Courageous Conversations. It's how you reclaim the ability to move forward with clarity instead of confusion, acting from truth instead of fear.

When I worked in corporate communications, I led a team of more than one hundred internal consultants. I met with my five direct reports weekly for one-on-one updates. One day, before a meeting, an inspired thought came to me. I said to an employee, "We're both stuck inside so much for meetings. How about we go for a walk outside instead?"

The "walking meeting" was born. My other direct reports started having walking meetings with me too. While we walked outdoors, I guided and coached them in navigating their challenges and opportunities related to their own employees and clients. Afterward we both felt clear, refreshed, and motivated for the rest of the day. Walking meetings were such a success that the idea caught on and spread throughout the organization.

When I founded Ascend Leadership Co., I brought this strategy with me and adapted it to be a "walking meeting with myself" where nature helps guide me on issues and opportunities that I'm navigating in my business and life. A cornerstone of my personal Entrepreneurial Time Rhythm is a thirty-minute walking meeting in the morning, usually around eight o'clock. Instead of *trying* to figure things out, things get figured out while I'm walking. My body feels good, and my mind becomes clear. Then, when I get back to my desk, I capture all the clarity that came to me.

Reading this, you may be saying, "Hey, Nadine, I'm already extremely busy. There's no way I have time for this." Believe me, I get it. There are still days when I resist it too. I remember one morning when I was overwhelmed and in tears. My to-do list felt crushing, and the last thing I wanted to do was go outside for a walk. I told Derek I couldn't afford the time. He gently looked at me and said, "You can't afford not to. Use your own medicine." Then he put his hand gently on my back and nudged me toward the door.

I didn't want to go, but I did. And within ten minutes of walking, breathing, and being in nature, the tears stopped. My nervous system settled. By the time I got back to my office, the knot in my chest had loosened, and my mind was clear again. I knew the decisions I needed to make, why they mattered, and what I was choosing for each one. That one walk unlocked a day of focused, aligned, strategic work. Not in spite of stepping away, but because of it.

These thirty minutes are the highest ROI time of the day for my business, and the bonus is it also helps me get clarity in my personal life too. What possibilities and opportunities might you unlock if you were to expand your understanding of productive time, work, and leadership? This is exactly what we help our clients explore.

Before working with Ascend Leadership Co., Katie Phillips, the owner of a premier consulting company for project management and organizational change professionals, measured her value by the number of hours she spent at her desk. If she wasn't glued to her computer or powering through back-to-back meetings, it didn't feel like real work. But that mindset was leaving her disconnected from the parts of her business she once loved.

"Before meeting Nadine and Derek, my business was taking a toll on my family, health, and personal life," Katie reflected. "I had started to resent it, yet every time I turned off my computer, I would feel guilty that I didn't get enough done that day. I didn't have a social life. I wasn't taking care of myself and started to see that it was impacting my health. I knew I needed to make a change and couldn't continue as I was."

With our help, Katie began to reconnect with her Wild Wisdom, the instinctive knowing that lives beyond computers and offices. As she tapped back into that intuitive sense of what truly matters, she strengthened her Time Mastery and began to build a more United Team. She embraced midday walking meetings, sparking creativity and strategy instead of draining her energy. She reframed what it meant to be a leader: not someone who's always "on," but someone who knows how to tune in, for both the present and the future.

This internal shift changed everything. Katie found her voice and self-trust as a leader and her Entrepreneurial Time Rhythm as a business owner and woman with a full life. In just one year, she saw meaningful growth while also spending more time with loved ones and friends, as well as falling back in love with her work.

"I now have my passion back for my business," she said. "I spend more time on myself and my health. I have more time with my family and see friends more often. I spend my weekends doing what I love, like being out in the mountains. I know what's of value to me, and I have time for all that matters."

Katie also embraced a new level of ownership over her calendar and energy. "I now have control over my time," she shared. "I've made the mindset shift that I have control over the things I do and when I do them. I have control over what and to whom I delegate and no longer get sucked into the wrong things."

That clarity removed the time guilt that used to follow Katie around. "I no longer feel guilty if I choose to work a long day because my work no longer overtakes every aspect of my life. I still have that control. To my kids and my husband, I demonstrate my passion for my business and not the resentment and hard feelings that I was feeling before. They're in my corner and on my side and want my business to succeed as well."

By trusting her Wild Wisdom, Katie stopped measuring success by the hours she worked at her desk and started leading from a place of alignment, clarity, and joy. Her personal transformation also translated into business strategy. "I now have a five-year plan for my business," she explained. "Prior to working with Nadine and Derek, I had blinders on and could only clearly think eight to ten months into the future."

Katie's story is proof that when leaders reclaim their Wild Wisdom, they don't just build better businesses—they build better lives.

# THE JOURNEY THROUGH FEAR
# TO SELF-TRUST

Getting to a place where you can be in tune with your Wild Wisdom isn't always comfortable. In fact, it often starts with discomfort. Fear is the gatekeeper to Wild Wisdom. It shows up as perfectionism, people-pleasing, impostor syndrome, or anxiety. Many leaders fear the consequences of slowing down or pausing, even for as little as thirty minutes a day. They worry about judgment, about getting it wrong, or about what they might discover if they stop long enough to listen to their inner wisdom.

Derek and I meet you there as you struggle within the Middle Zone. The first step in accessing Wild Wisdom is acknowledging your present fears. We create space for you to recognize and voice your concerns, asking questions like, "What fears are coming up for you? What is this fear telling you?" The most common fears we encounter from leaders include:

- Worry about others' opinions of them.
- Doubt about their own competence to make and follow through on decisions.
- Perfectionism and fear of making wrong choices.

We start with your fear and validate it. Because fear isn't the enemy; it's a messenger. And when strong leaders like you feel seen and supported in your fear, a shift happens. You begin to remember who you are. You reconnect with the quiet confidence and inherent resourcefulness beneath the chaos. And you start making decisions from self-trust instead of fear. Let's return to the story of Susie of Ramar Foods.

Susie stood at a pivotal crossroads. On paper she was successfully leading a legacy business, meeting her responsibilities, and managing her team. But underneath, the pressure was unrelenting. Her business was consuming her time, energy, and joy. She was stuck in the Middle Zone, doing everything she was supposed to do, yet feeling disconnected from herself and the life she wanted to live.

We worked with Susie to build her Time Mastery and close the leadership leaks that were preventing her from building a United Team, but something was missing and calling for her attention. When we started exploring Susie's Wild Wisdom, a different truth emerged. Susie lit up when she spoke about nature. Hiking, walking outdoors, and moving her body in fresh air weren't just hobbies for her. They were lifelines. And she had been sacrificing them in the name of business growth and responsibility.

I gave Susie a gentle invitation: "It's time to return to Mother Nature."

What started as a simple morning walk became a turning point. Susie began to prioritize time in nature not as a break from work, but as a way of reconnecting with herself and accessing her inner knowing. Her walks became sacred to her. They slowed her mind. They settled her body. They calmed her nervous system. In that stillness, Susie's Wild Wisdom, the part of her that knew what mattered, began to resurface. The clarity she had been chasing in meetings and metrics began showing up among the trees and the trails. She no longer felt like she had to hustle for every answer. Instead, the clearest answers naturally came to her as she started hearing her own inner voice again—steady, quiet, trustworthy.

This wasn't just about movement or mindfulness. It was about trading fear for self-trust. Susie realized she could approach her leadership from two radically different places:

frantic obligation or grounded presence. She chose presence. When she committed to making her morning nature walks nonnegotiable, Susie also committed to redesigning her entire approach to her work and life. She was breaking free from the "shoulds" and external expectations that had been suffocating her authentic self.

The impact rippled outward. Susie's nature walks became a business strategy for accessing her Wild Wisdom. Her energy shifted. Her team noticed. She showed up in her business calmer, clearer, and more aligned. Her nature walks weren't a detour from leadership; they were the foundation of it. Susie's story reminds us that Wild Wisdom doesn't need to be earned through hardship. It needs to be remembered through ease and joy. For her, that remembrance began with lacing up her shoes, stepping outside, and letting nature guide her back to the self she'd nearly forgotten but never truly lost.

Wild Wisdom is not one-size-fits-all. It doesn't require a mountain hike or a weeklong retreat (although, as you'll see below, retreats can be life-changing too). It simply requires you to find the form of nature that speaks to you and taps into your inner compass, knowing, and intuition. For some, it's a walk in the woods. For others, it's found in a garden or greenhouse, or kayaking on a lake, or skiing along a trail.

The key is embodiment and accessing the wisdom below your shoulders. When you walk barefoot on the earth, or breathe deeply with the trees, or let the wind move through your hair, you return to your true nature. And in that space, you hear an inner voice that's always been there. You realize the clarity you seek isn't somewhere out there beyond your reach. It's already inside you, and it's been there all along. You just need the right conditions to access it.

# THE CALL OF KALALAU

My access to Wild Wisdom began long before I had a name for it. I spent most of my childhood outside, racing around on my motorbike, building adventures with sandboxes and wheelbarrows, and playing with our dogs, cats, and horses. My mom could hardly get me inside for supper. I felt most alive when I was moving, exploring, and surrounded by nature. Even indoors, I found ways to create and express my individual nature, like rearranging my bedroom for fun or getting lost in cross-stitch projects passed down from my grandmother.

Looking back, the first ten years of my life were pure magic. I was deeply connected to my instincts, creativity, and the natural world. And while adulthood brought new kinds of joy like motherhood, founding my own business, and intentionally designing a life of Impossible Freedom that allows me to spend time in sacred places like Lake O'Hara, that early connection to nature is where my deep understanding of Wild Wisdom comes from. Years later, in one of the wildest places on earth, my Wild Wisdom called to me louder than ever with the help of Mother Nature.

In 2001, before Derek and I got married, we spent three weeks on vacation on the Hawaiian Islands. We hired a helicopter to see the Nāpali Coast State Wilderness Park on the island of Kauai. Flying above the magnificent natural landscape, I took in the sheer beauty and energy of the land below. The pristine waters and soaring mountains, draped in vegetation, stretched toward the horizon. I was in tears, overcome with gratitude, awe, and serenity. Peering down, we discovered the formidable Kalalau Trail threading along the coastline.

The Kalalau Trail is no ordinary hike. As one of Kauai's most protected and challenging backpacking adventures, it is eleven miles long one way, making the round trip twenty-two miles. While the trail's start and end points are at sea level, the constant ups and downs along the rugged landscape result in a total elevation gain of about sixty-five hundred feet. To hike the full eleven-mile trail, you're required to get a permit, and at the time the state government only issued fifty permits a day.

The next day, after the helicopter ride, we hiked the first two miles of the trail, which are accessible to the general public. After seeing it from so far above, feeling my feet on that path was a spiritual experience connecting sky to earth. At the end of the hike, I pulled out my camera, took a photo of the beautiful landscape, and told Derek, "One day I'm going to return to hike this entire path."

Sixteen years later, while on a walking meeting with myself at home in Calgary, that long ago promise resurfaced and became an ambitious vision. Not content to only fulfill my personal dream, I felt called to share this experience with other entrepreneurs. I decided to lead a one-week business retreat on the Kalalau Trail, called the Rise Up Retreat™. Spots on the retreat filled within days. When we're aligned with our inner spirit and deeper purpose, life moves swiftly to support us.

At forty-six years old, I found myself leading five entrepreneurs on a grueling journey that would test not only my physical limits, but also my understanding of leadership and wisdom. We spent our first night together in Lihue, the closest town to the airport. At four o'clock in the morning, our mountain guide picked us up and drove us to the trailhead an hour and a half away. Although each hiker was ultimately responsible for their own safety, I hired the guide to ensure we got through the hike as safely as possible.

Over the course of thirteen long hours, we forged through lush jungle and rough terrain, including the heart-stopping

Crawler's Ledge, an eighteen-inch-wide cliff path with a twenty-five-hundred-foot drop-off to the Pacific Ocean below. We trekked up and down extreme elevation gains and losses, pushing ourselves to our limits. When the sun set, we had only covered eight of the trail's eleven miles. It would be too dangerous to keep going in the dark, so we made camp for the night in Hanakoa Valley. The next day, we finished the remaining three miles and reached our destination: Kalalau Beach.

As soon as we arrived where we would set up our beachside camp, I dropped my forty-pound backpack and felt a calling to take the two-minute walk to the beach. Kalalau Beach is private and intimate, wild and serene. The waters are dangerous, with a strong undertow that can kill. Swimming is not allowed there, as is accessing the beach by boat due to strict marine regulations and the harsh natural conditions in the area. The only access is by backpacking in on foot.

I had just finished the hardest hike of my life. I was in good shape physically, yet it had still challenged my strength, stamina, and endurance. Reaching the end of the trail was a dream come true. I'd wanted this for years, and I'd finally done it. It was an accomplishment of a lifetime. The beach was sweeping, expansive, its sand soft and fluffy, the waters turquoise and clear. It was framed by the towering sea cliffs of the Nāpali Coast, steep grassy ridges, and a field of rugged boulders.

Turning to stand with my back to the ocean, my initial elation melted away, and I felt the weight of responsibility crash over me. I had led plenty of business retreats before but always in luxurious backcountry lodges in the Canadian Rocky Mountains, and often with Derek as my co-leader. Here, miles from civilization, without any backup, self-doubt crept into me like the evening tide.

*What was I thinking, bringing these people to such a remote location and making promises to lead them in transformation?*

Suddenly, I felt lonely—while also wishing I was there by myself, responsible only for myself. The stress of having an entire group of people look to me for guidance in the wild outdoors was extraordinary. Our mountain guide had gotten us safely to the campsite at Kalalau Beach, and he would handle the cooking, but it was my turn to lead the rest of the retreat. Everything else fell on my shoulders. While I had planned the retreat and knew I needed to deliver, the passion and confidence I'd started the adventure with fled. I felt paralyzed about how to move forward. I had never led a business retreat completely outside, in the middle of a Hawaiian jungle, with only tents to sleep in and no lodge accommodations. Derek wasn't there to provide me a safety net. I felt exposed and alone.

As I tilted my head back, gazing up at the wide-open blue sky and sharp mountain peaks piercing the jungle canopy, a message came to me with startling clarity: *You are not alone. I am your co-facilitator.*

In that moment, Mother Nature herself clearly spoke to me, telling me she was my partner, not only on that retreat, but in the rest of my life too. She always had my back. She was with me. Just like I did at home in Canada, I could trust her to support me through every obstacle and challenge I encountered here in Kauai. The realization washed away my fears, replacing them with a deep sense of knowing and purpose.

Over the next four days, our group collected firewood, meditated beneath the stars, bathed in sacred waterfalls, and journaled in the embrace of wilderness. We walked barefoot and became one with the land. We shared our dreams around the campfire and practiced yoga near a sacred heiau, an ancient Hawaiian temple, with humpback whales serenading us.

We relaxed on the soft, sandy beach, and I guided everyone to create clear plans to grow their businesses and their lives of Impossible Freedom.

Without the distractions of technology or personal and professional obligations, each leader connected deeply with their own Wild Wisdom. They faced fears, pushed beyond discomfort, and opened themselves to new possibilities, potential, and action. We were co-creating with Mother Nature.

The experience reconfirmed what I had long known: Being in nature provides a direct pathway to our deepest truth, inner spirit, knowledge, and intuition. When we step into the wild, we connect with our spirit in ways that transcend ordinary understanding. Looking up at the towering wilderness of Kalalau, listening to the wind in the trees, smelling the salt-laced air, I felt simultaneously humbled—a single grain of sand in the vastness of our earth—and extraordinarily empowered by my connection to a power greater than myself.

This is the essence of Wild Wisdom: recognizing that nature is both our teacher and our partner in leadership and life. Whether you're standing on a remote beach or making decisions in a boardroom, that connection to your wild inner knowing remains your most reliable guide. In other words, nature is a shortcut to our truth, if you have the courage to answer her call.

## WHY WILD WISDOM COMES FIRST

Wild Wisdom is the first of the Leadership Amplifiers for a reason. It's the fuel that makes everything else possible. Without it, decisions are reactive and fear-based. Conversations are hesitant or postponed. Time and team fall into disarray. But when you're grounded in Wild Wisdom, you move through business and life with conviction and calm. You make Brave Decisions.

You initiate Courageous Conversations. You model clarity for your team and prioritize your time as the nonrenewable resource it is. Wild Wisdom helps eliminate your Say/Do Gap and Support Gap because you're no longer making promises that aren't true or agreeing to things out of obligation. You're leading from inner truth, and inner truth is always aligned.

At Ascend Leadership Co., we work with founders and CEOs whose companies generate anywhere from seven to nine figures in annual revenue, and every one of them comes to us over-thinking, overworking, feeling paralyzed, or experiencing decision fatigue, regardless of how much money they make. After working with us, our clients come to see time in nature as their number one business strategy and a nonnegotiable pillar of their leadership. When they get out in nature, business clarity emerges not because they're trying harder, but because they're not trying. They're listening. They're feeling. They're trusting nature—and who they are in nature—to lead them where they need to go.

Because those who wander in nature find themselves.

In this chapter, we've explored how reconnecting with your Wild Wisdom begins with tuning in, really tuning in, to your inner voice to clear away the clutter that keeps you stuck in the Middle Zone. You've seen how nature isn't just restorative; it's perspective-shifting and truth-revealing. It shows you what truly matters and what you already know. It calms your nervous system so you can hear what your intuition has been whispering all along. Whether it's a walk around the block, a weekend hike, time in your garden, or a business retreat into the wild, the tools that reconnect you to your inner knowing are simple, accessible, and powerful. Breath work, walking meetings, journaling in nature, morning solitude, and other embodied practices all help bring your body and spirit back into alignment with your truth, your leadership, and your power.

When you make space for these practices and listen deeply, you start to make decisions not from fear but from self-trust. You stop chasing external validation and unhelpful metrics, like the number of hours spent at your desk, and start leading from a place of calm confidence. You begin clearing away distractions and honoring what's essential. And you remember, deep in your bones, that you already know the way. You just need space to hear it.

This is the quiet, unwavering power of Wild Wisdom, the power that leads you out of the Middle Zone and toward Impossible Freedom, where trade-offs and self-sacrifice are no longer the cost of achievement. It doesn't shout. It doesn't demand. But it's always speaking. All you have to do is pause, listen, and follow.

**Your First Wild Wisdom Practice:** If you're feeling stuck, start here. Start now.

Step outside—into a park, a backyard, a stretch of trail. Leave your phone behind. Walk for at least twenty minutes (thirty minutes is ideal). No podcast. No music. No agenda. No email. No striving.

Just walk. Just listen. Feel your feet connecting with the earth. Feel the rhythm of your breath. Notice what stirs within you.

Ask yourself:

"What do I want?"

"What do I value?"

"What is deeply true for me?"

"What is wanting to happen?"

Then listen. Really listen. The quiet knowing, *that* is your Wild Wisdom. It's already within you. It always has been. And it will lead you exactly where you're meant to go.

# YOUR REFLECT TO RISE JOURNAL

**Wild Wisdom Reconnection:** This chapter frames Wild Wisdom as a leadership and business strategy, not just an inner voice. When have you experienced a moment of deep knowing or intuition in your work or life? How did it shape your next steps?

**The Nature Shortcut:** Nature is described as the fastest way to access your inner clarity. What types of nature (external or internal) have helped you feel most grounded and connected? How might you bring more of that into your routine, even in small ways?

**From Fear to Self-Trust:** Fear is the gatekeeper to Wild Wisdom. What fears currently show up when you consider slowing down, regularly stepping away from your desk, or listening inward? What stories or beliefs do those fears stem from?

**Embodied Practice:** Chapter 4 shares several embodied practices and rituals that can be integrated into your Entrepreneurial Time Rhythm, including physical activity (especially outdoors), meditation, prayer, yoga, gardening, spiritual verse reading, breath work, journaling, morning solitude, and walking meetings. What's one embodied or nature-based practice you could experiment with this week to access more clarity and alignment?

**Taking Action:** Which of your current business challenges might benefit from Wild Wisdom instead of more effort or analysis? What's one decision or next step you could allow to emerge rather than force?

**Community Connection:** How can you show up in community while staying connected to your Wild Wisdom? What boundaries or practices help you stay true to yourself, even when others have different opinions or expectations?

## CHAPTER 5

# BRAVE DECISIONS: CONFIDENCE IN MOTION

*By Derek Nicholson*

N adine and I have each faced moments when the "right" choice on paper felt deeply wrong in our gut. In Chapter 2, she shared her decision to leave corporate life after her father's passing. For me, one defining Brave Decision came a few years later—a moment that taught me what it truly means to trust your inner knowing, even when the stakes are high.

In 2018, after a two-year sabbatical from corporate life, I was headhunted for what most people in my former industry, healthcare sales, would call a dream job. It came with a prestigious title, a $300,000 compensation package, plus travel perks, a company car, a generous healthcare plan, and more. That kind of offer doesn't come around often, especially in Western Canada; most of these opportunities are based in head offices in Ontario in Eastern Canada. By all external measures, it was everything I'd been working toward in my career.

So I said yes.

And within six days, I chose to walk away.

On paper the role was perfect. Deep down, though, I realized I had accepted it from a place of fear. Fear that nothing better would come along. Fear that I couldn't let anyone down. Fear that I had to provide financial stability for our family. I thought I was being responsible, but after some deep reflection, I realized I had ignored my inner knowing, instincts, and truth (the Wild Wisdom we explored in Chapter 4).

The job didn't align with how I wanted to lead or live or even how I believed the role should be performed. The company expected me to spend an inordinate amount of time entering data into a spreadsheet and preparing weekly PowerPoint presentations to report progress toward statistical goals. I'm a relationship guy. I thrive in getting out there and building relationships with clients and potential clients, not being weighed down by excessive administration. And I know relationships are what ultimately drive business results and success; I've demonstrated that over and over in my career. Yet this company was not looking for that from me. More than that, I realized I was chasing what society and the industry expected of me, not what my heart wanted.

This wasn't the first time our family had been faced with a big, shiny offer that didn't match the life we were trying to build. Back in 2011, not long after Nadine launched her business, she was offered a $350,000 communications manager role at a prestigious oil company. It was a job she could do in her sleep with an incredible financial upside. After some soul-searching and support from her United Team, she turned it down. She knew her vision for her business, and her desire to help others build businesses and lives aligned with their values, mattered more than a title or consistent paycheck.

Watching her make that decision planted a seed in me. When it was my turn to choose years later, I had a model for what bravery looked like.

Resigning from that management position wasn't easy for me. I didn't have a backup plan. But I trusted that letting go of something misaligned with what I truly wanted would make space for something better. Eventually, that led me to partner with Nadine and help rebrand her business to Ascend Leadership Co., where we now co-lead with purpose and partnership instead of pressure and paperwork.

During that six-day detour, I had one of the clearest conversations I've ever had with my Wild Wisdom. It told me to let this opportunity go. I listened, and it led me to one of the best, bravest decisions I've ever made. That's what this chapter is about: Brave Decisions, the second Leadership Amplifier in the Impossible Freedom Equation. Brave Decisions aren't always loud or dramatic. Sometimes they unfold quietly in late-night conversations, hotel rooms, or coaching sessions. They begin with a whisper from within, a sense that something's off, or a tug toward a different path. When you listen and act on that inner knowing, everything begins to shift.

In this chapter, you'll meet leaders who stood at similar crossroads. Each leader, including Nadine, faced high-stakes decisions that demanded more than pure, unemotional logic. They also required courage, self-trust, and clarity. Their stories offer real-life examples of how Brave Decisions can break cycles of fear, reclaim agency, and ignite momentum. Through these stories of transformation, you'll see how aligned choices don't only change circumstances. They also change people. And you'll begin to see how the same is possible for you.

## THE HEART OF THE BRAVE DECISION

A Brave Decision is a bold, confident choice rooted in your inner wisdom—not in external validation, pressure, or expectations. It's not just about doing something that feels hard. It's about making the best decision for you, one that aligns with who you truly are, even when the stakes are high, the risks are real, and the path ahead is uncertain. At its core, a Brave Decision is a conscious pivot out of fear and into self-trust.

In our Impossible Freedom Equation, Brave Decisions sit between Wild Wisdom (your inner knowing) and Courageous Conversations (the communication about your decision that follows). Brave Decisions are what turn clarity into commitment. They're the activation point of your vision. Without them, you delay. You swirl in indecision. You leak time, energy, and confidence.

When you step out of the Middle Zone (where things are unsustainable and unfulfilling), you begin to make choices from a place of deep rootedness, and everything shifts. You build momentum. You grow self-trust. You escape chronic cycles of indecision, decision fatigue, overanalysis, and overwhelm. You scale your business with inner wisdom and step onto the path toward Impossible Freedom.

Nadine's experience guiding one of our clients, Stef, through a Brave Decision illustrates one way we support our clients. You first met her in Chapter 1. Stef arrived at her executive leadership coaching meeting with Nadine exhausted. She'd been losing sleep, stuck in a period of overthinking and second-guessing herself. Five major issues were weighing on her, each one tangled in conflicting advice and noisy opinions. Some came from colleagues and team members, some from hired consultants, and many from inside her own head. She was disconnected from her body, gripped by fear, and unsure what to do or even how to think about what she was facing.

Nadine guided her through a body-based process, beginning with a simple shaking exercise to release tension and help Stef return to her inner wisdom. Then came a visualization. With her eyes closed, Stef slowly tuned out external voices and tuned into her Wild Wisdom. One by one, Nadine walked her through each issue, asking, "What's your truth? Not what others think—what do you believe?" Stef answered with growing clarity. With every response, her confidence became stronger.

One of Stef's most pressing issues concerned a branding consultant who insisted that Stef had to choose what Ripplea should be known for: strategy or implementation. The message was: "If you try to be both, you're trying to be everything for everyone." Those words had been echoing in Stef's head for days. But in the quiet and calm of her meeting with Nadine, Stef saw through the binary. The truth was unequivocal: Her company's strength lay in its ability to do both strategy and implementation. That's what made Ripplea different.

By the end of their hour-long session (most of which Stef spent with her eyes closed in embodied clarity work), she had completely transformed. The shift was visible. She went from scattered and unsure to grounded and confident. From disconnected to fully rooted in her body. From overthinking every angle to having 100 percent conviction in her truth, knowledge, and wisdom. Not only did Stef know what to do, but she also knew how to communicate her decisions to her United Team, including her branding consultant.

**Key Takeaways from Stef's Story:**

- Embodiment unlocks clarity: Stef's shift from overthinking to confidence started with returning to her body through breath, movement, and visualization.
- Inner truth outweighs external pressure: Even when a consultant pushed a binary choice, Stef's Wild Wisdom revealed a third path aligned with her company's true strength.
- Decision-making is identity work: By claiming her truth, Stef didn't only solve a business problem; she stepped into her leadership with renewed conviction.
- Brave Decisions ripple outward: Stef's inner knowing empowered her to lead her team with confidence and maintain alignment with her brand vision.

## THE RIDGEWALK: HOW BRAVE DECISIONS COME TO LIFE

Brave Decisions don't happen in a vacuum. They happen on the Ridgewalk.

The Ridgewalk is what we call the core decision-making process that moves founders and CEOs out of the Middle Zone toward Impossible Freedom. It's how Stef shifted from overthinking and paralysis into confidence and conviction. It's not a single moment or tactic. It's a way of being. A way of navigating decision points with integrity, clarity, and truth.

Picture it like this: You're on a path walking up a mountain. The Middle Zone is halfway up. At the top is Impossible Freedom. The path that connects the two is the Ridgewalk, and the two most important levers that determine how you move along the Ridgewalk are time and team. How you invest your time and whom you bring with you either accelerate your momentum or keep you trapped in the Middle Zone.

The Ridgewalk gets its name from this powerful metaphor. On either side of the path up the mountain are opposing forces. One side is fear, scarcity, and past programming—the voices of obligation, pressure, and what others expect. The other side is self-trust, possibility, and truth—your deepest values, vision, and self-knowledge. Every decision you make, every action you take, can come from either side of the path. The Ridgewalk is a systematic way of holding space for both sides, acknowledging the fear and voices that pull you back while still choosing your decisions and actions from your Wild Wisdom, where self-trust lives.

This is the heart of Brave Decisions: They aren't just about what you do; they're about who you're *being* when you choose. Two people can take the same tactical action (e.g., pivot a business, hire a new team member, negotiate an offer), but if one does it from the energy of fear and the other from the energy of self-trust, the outcomes will be entirely different. One reinforces doubt and stagnation. The other creates momentum and strength.

You're likely standing in a Ridgewalk moment when you feel stuck or torn, second-guessing yourself with no clear or confident next move. There's urgency in the air, pressure to act fast, yet your gut says, *Wait.* The fear shows up disguised as logic or responsibility: *Be practical. Play it safe. Don't let anyone down.* You may find yourself trying to make everyone else happy while ignoring your own needs. These moments are often invisible to others, but they define your journey and trajectory.

The Ridgewalk helps you recognize both the importance and opportunity of these moments. As a repeatable process, it gently prompts you to remember that making the right decision always comes from a place of self-trust and inner truth.

It harnesses the power of all three Leadership Amplifiers—Wild Wisdom, Brave Decisions, and Courageous Conversations—in a sequence that transforms clarity into energy and reframes uncertainty and limitation as possibility. Think of the Leadership Amplifiers as the supports beneath your feet. The more consistently you use them, the stronger and more stable the path becomes. Without them, the Ridgewalk erodes, leaving you vulnerable to slipping back into the Middle Zone.

The Ridgewalk decision-making process flows through three key steps:

1. **Get Clear on Your Inner Truth (Wild Wisdom):** This step usually requires a pause, an intentional break from external noise and the voices of fear. It might look like a nature walk, journaling, or simply a few deep breaths to reinhabit your body. The goal is to quiet the outside voices and reconnect with your inner knowing. For Stef, it meant closing her eyes, tuning out the mental clutter, and listening inward. One by one, she named her truths. Her Wild Wisdom had been there all along; she just hadn't been able to hear, feel, or trust it.

2. **Make the Brave Decision:** From this rooted, clear place, you decide. Not reactively. Not out of obligation. But with conviction. This is the moment you stop outsourcing your decisions and start owning what's right for you. In Stef's case, she stopped questioning herself and declared her company's unique strength: delivering both strategy and implementation. Despite the consultant's expertise, Stef was the ultimate expert on her own inner truth. She finally claimed that as part of her identity.

3. **Communicate Your Decision with Courage (Courageous Conversations):** Once the decision is made, it needs to be shared with kindness and firmness with those who

are impacted. Whether you're informing others, setting a boundary, or stepping in a bold new direction, courageous communication brings the decision to life. Stef left her session with Nadine knowing exactly what to do and fully ready to express it in a way that would honor her decision while keeping the branding consultant as part of her United Team. She walked away firmly planted in her message, clear on her path, and no longer second-guessing.

Each of the steps in the Ridgewalk builds on the one before it. Together they form a powerful upward spiral that strengthens your self-trust, amplifies your leadership, and moves you closer to Impossible Freedom at the top of the mountain. The Ridgewalk doesn't end after one decision. Because it's a spiral, every step forward generates more momentum. You begin to see evidence of alignment. Your confidence builds. And with each new challenge, you come at it from a higher vantage point. Even when things don't go to plan, the focus is no longer on failure. Instead, it's on learning and growth.

But the spiral can also move in the other direction. When your decisions come from fear, scarcity, or self-doubt, they tend to compound. You stall out. You overthink. You second-guess. Over time this creates a quiet, downward spiral that erodes your confidence and keeps you stuck. That's why the Ridgewalk exists: to break that pattern and offer a new way forward. Even if your last decision came from fear, your next one doesn't have to.

Most leaders unknowingly make 80 percent or more of their decisions from the energy of fear, scarcity, obligation, pressure, and what others expect. Only a small fraction of their decisions, 20 percent or less, comes from the energy of self-trust, possibility, confidence, and inner truth. The Ridgewalk flips that ratio. It equips you to act unwaveringly from alignment, not reaction. To use time and team intentionally. To move toward the summit of Impossible Freedom with increasing certainty and strength. When you learn to take the Ridgewalk, you don't only lead your business and life differently. You also become someone different. Someone who trusts herself. Someone who makes bold moves without apology. Someone who turns clarity into commitment and walks the path to achieve Impossible Freedom, one Brave Decision at a time.

## BREAKING FREE FROM FEAR-BASED PARALYSIS

The relationship between fear and decision-making can either keep you stuck or become a catalyst for transformation. In Chapter 4, you learned that fear is the gatekeeper to accessing your Wild Wisdom. As part of the Ridgewalk, that means it also gatekeeps Brave Decisions. When a founder or CEO doubts herself and feels paralyzed by fear around a decision she knows she needs to make, we encourage her to pause and get curious about the fear. What is it really about? Where is it really coming from? Why does it feel so debilitating right now?

Once she feels seen, heard, and acknowledged, we guide her to identify one action that will resurface her self-trust and inner knowing. This action could be any of the embodied practices discussed in Chapter 4. Once she feels more grounded and centered, we guide her through the Ridgewalk to . . .

- Gain clarity on her inner truth related to the issue.
- Make a Brave Decision aligned with that truth.
- Prepare to courageously communicate her decision to those involved.

This process ensures she moves forward with confidence and alignment instead of from a place of fear. Let's see it in action, with more detail.

Katie Bigelow, the president of a defense technology company, found herself at a critical turning point. As her company grew past eight figures in revenue, she realized trying to manage both high-level leadership and day-to-day operations was no longer sustainable. She needed to hire an operations manager, yet she remained paralyzed by overthinking and fear.

Her mind filled with doubts: *What if I hire the wrong person? What if the team resists the change? What if the right candidate doesn't exist?* These concerns kept Katie from acting, despite knowing deep down that bringing in the right person would free her to focus on strategic leadership and business growth.

Katie's hesitation is not unique. Many high-performing leaders face the same internal resistance, even when they know a change is needed. This is especially true when the change involves growing their team, handing off work, and letting go of control. The fear of making the wrong decision, disappointing others, or venturing into the unknown can stall even the most successful leader.

Through executive leadership coaching with Ascend Leadership Co., Katie learned to shift her mindset from fear-based paralysis to confident decision-making. She followed a structured process, with the Ridgewalk at its heart, to move forward:

1. **Recognize the Fear:** Instead of letting fear control her actions, Katie acknowledged her worries and named them. Identifying the root of her hesitation helped lessen its grip.
2. **Clarify What You Want:** Rather than focusing on what could go wrong, she tapped into her own Wild Wisdom and defined

what the right hire would look like. What qualities would the hire need? What values should they embody? What kind of positive impact would they have on the team and company?

3.  **Visualize Success and Gratitude:** Katie imagined the ideal scenario—an operations manager who thrived in their role, alleviating her workload and contributing to the company's long-term vision. She allowed herself to feel the relief and gratitude that would come with making the right hire.

4.  **Make the Brave Decision:** Grounded in clarity and alignment, Katie committed to moving forward with the hire. She chose to believe in her leadership, her vision for the company, and the resources at her disposal.

5.  **Recognize Existing Opportunities:** Katie realized the right person might already be within her network. Instead of waiting for the perfect candidate to magically appear, she proactively reviewed her contacts, reached out to her peers, and asked for referrals.

6.  **Take Action:** With newfound confidence, Katie began the hiring process in earnest, engaging with potential candidates and trusting herself to make a well-informed decision. This step also included Courageous Conversations and reinforced her role as a strategic leader.

By shifting her focus from uncertainty to possibility, Katie broke free from her paralyzing cycle of fear and overthinking. She trusted her instincts and ultimately transformed both her leadership role and the company's future. Katie's story serves as a powerful lesson. Fear and doubt may always be present, but they don't have to dictate your decisions. The key to growth, both personal and professional, is learning to acknowledge the fear, get clear on what you truly want, and take courageous steps forward.

**Key Takeaways from Katie's Story:**

- Fear often masks clarity: Katie's paralysis around hiring stemmed not from a lack of options, but from a fear of making the wrong move.
- Specificity calms the nervous system: Naming her fears and clearly defining the kind of hire she wanted helped reduce overwhelm and restore momentum.
- Visualization shifts mindset: Imagining success and gratitude helped Katie anchor into a future worth moving toward, instead of reacting to what could go wrong.
- Action breaks the cycle: Intentional communication (reaching out to her network) was the catalyst for moving from stuck to solution.
- Empowered hiring is brave leadership: By trusting her instincts, Katie freed herself to lead more strategically and scale her business from a place of inner alignment.

## MOVING BEYOND THE TRADE-OFF MINDSET

Sometimes the most defining decisions are the ones you make side by side with another member of your United Team, when you have no clear road map and everything is on the line. Let me tell you a story about a Ridgewalk moment that Nadine faced and I shared as her partner. It was 2016, and I was at the beginning of my two-year sabbatical from corporate life. Nadine was carrying the financial weight of our household and growing her company. I felt like money was tight, and we needed to defer some of our dreams. Then a new opportunity emerged and, with it, a decision that demanded self-trust, clarity, and courage.

Nadine felt a deep pull to hire two transformational coaches, Tracey and George. Their yearlong program promised significant growth for Nadine and her business, but the investment was steep—three times higher than she had ever spent on coaching for herself. It involved travel, accommodation, and time away from the business's day-to-day operations. Logically, it didn't make sense. But her Wild Wisdom said otherwise.

Nadine flew to Los Angeles to attend one of Tracey and George's live events to get a feel for their energy in person. In her words, she didn't want to commit without "looking them in the eye." During one of their workshops, the coaches asked participants to get honest about what they wanted most. Nadine texted me from the room, asking me the same question.

Without hesitation, I replied: "I've always wanted a BMW M3." Nadine showered me with support and said I should go for it.

The dream of owning a BMW M3 had been with me since I was a kid and wanted to become a race car driver. As an adult, I was drawn to the M3 because it's considered both a racetrack-ready car and a family sedan. Still, at that moment, owning one felt impossibly far away.

Meanwhile, Nadine was wrestling with her own fears related to making the financial investment in coaching. Alone in her two-bed hotel room that night, she faced a dark night of the soul. Her thoughts raced. Doubt crept in.

Then Nadine's intuition nudged her toward her Wild Wisdom. *Take a bath*, it whispered. *Connect with your feminine side.* After the bath, as Nadine was trying to fall asleep again, she received another message from her inner spirit telling her to switch beds. The sheets on the unused bed were crisp and fresh, her body cooled down, and she dropped into sleep quickly.

By morning, Nadine was clear. She knew what she wanted to do. Now it was time to bring me into her decision-making process. That's where the next part of the Ridgewalk came in. This was the conversation that brought the Brave Decision to life.

When she called me, Nadine didn't push. She didn't try to convince me of anything. She simply spoke from her truth. "I'm really clear," she said. "I want to hire Tracey and George, but I know you haven't been here. You haven't experienced them like I have. You haven't seen what I've seen."

Nadine led us in a Courageous Conversation, bringing her decision to the table while making space for my experience too. I took a breath and responded honestly. "Nadine, I trust you. I know you're going to get the most out of this. You're growing the company, and I want us to invest in you. But . . . I won't get the car."

That was my first instinct: a zero-sum or trade-off mindset. One dream in, the other out. Nadine didn't accept that limitation. She replied with quiet conviction, "I truly believe we can invest in this coaching, and you can still get the car. I'm taking a stand for us having both." That one sentence shifted my perspective. Nadine didn't just believe in herself. She believed in our ability as a family to expand beyond false trade-offs. That, right there, was the Brave Decision. She committed to the coaching program. She chose growth, even in uncertainty. As it turns out, we were both right. The coaching experience was transformational and lucrative for Nadine. And, yes, I got the BMW M3, a car I still drive and love today.

This Ridgewalk moment became a touchstone for us. It taught us that trusting your Wild Wisdom doesn't mean the fear disappears. It means you move forward anyway while holding space for the fear. It taught us that Brave Decisions are not just about logic or timing, but about having the courage to invest in growth even when it feels risky. Most of all, it showed us that Impossible Freedom lives on the other side of limitation and trade-offs, if you're willing to walk toward it with clarity, conviction, and trust.

**Key Takeaways from our Story:**

- Growth requires investment, particularly when it's uncomfortable: Nadine's decision to pursue high-level coaching, despite temporary financial strain, showed that self-trust often asks for bold action.
- Intuition needs space to speak: Nadine's clarity came not from logic but from embodied intuition (a bath, a bed switch, and a deep inner pause).
- Courageous Conversations build trust: Our open, values-driven dialogue created shared understanding, even when trade-offs seemed inevitable.
- Vision expands possibility: Nadine refused the either/or mindset and held space for both the coaching investment and my dream car, redefining what was possible for us.
- Aligned decisions echo forward: This Brave Decision became a touchstone in our life and business, modeling what expansive, trust-based decision-making (and leadership) really looks like.

## TURNING HARD CHOICES INTO POWERFUL TURNING POINTS

It's time to return to Susie of Ramar Foods, whose journey we've been following since Chapter 1. Her story provides a powerful and unique example of how Brave Decisions come to life through the Ridgewalk, especially when the stakes are high, the path is uncertain, and the pressure to maintain the status quo feels overwhelming.

When Susie began coaching with us, she was carrying the invisible weight of legacy. As the leader of a multigenerational family business, she had inherited both a title and a culture of self-reliance and stoicism. "We don't need outside help. Figure it out yourself." That was the unspoken rule. So even considering executive leadership coaching felt like an indulgence and breach of company norms.

But Susie was facing mounting pressure. Her leadership team was burned out. Deadlines were slipping. Trust was fraying. And she was struggling with her own emotional reactivity in meetings, pulled between her desire for innovation and the pressure to preserve what had always been. In her heart and gut, she knew something needed to change. She just didn't know where to start.

That's when Susie made her first Brave Decision: to invest in herself as her number one asset. Choosing to work with us at Ascend Leadership Co. wasn't only about strategy or tactics. It was a symbolic shift. Susie stopped outsourcing her authority and began tuning into her own Wild Wisdom. (Return to Chapter 4 for more detail about this aspect of Susie's journey). She realized that if she wanted to lead differently, she had to be different. That clarity, rooted in self-trust and nature, became the foundation for pivotal decision-making.

One of Susie's biggest challenges was navigating changes within her leadership team. She had long sensed an organizational restructure was needed, but fear and uncertainty had kept her stuck. What if she made the wrong move? What if it damaged relationships or undermined morale? Through the Ridgewalk, Susie got clear on what she truly wanted: a leadership structure that supported the company's long-term vision and created space for innovation. With our support, she mapped her decisions from a source of truth and strength, not one of guilt, fear, or old patterns.

In one particularly difficult case, Susie realized a key team member was no longer a fit for their current role. However, that didn't mean they had to leave the company entirely. Instead of defaulting to a binary "stay or go" choice, Susie created a third path.

"I knew a leadership change needed to happen, but I wasn't sure how to approach it," she reflected. "With Nadine and Derek's guidance, I made the decision in a way that worked for both the company and the individual. It was a game changer."

This moment exemplified what it means to lead from alignment. By getting clear on her truth and committing to act from it, Susie was able to move through a potentially painful transition with kindness, firmness, grace, and care. The outcome was not only a better organizational structure, but also a stronger culture and a richer sense of trust and respect across the team.

Other Brave Decisions followed:

1. **Redesigning Her Calendar:** Like many leaders, Susie's schedule was driven by urgency rather than intention. She bravely restructured it, color-coding self-care and free time, strategic thinking, walking meetings with herself in nature, team leadership, and administrative time. This not only gave Susie visibility into how she was spending her energy, but also helped her recalibrate when misalignment crept in.

2. **Succession Planning:** For the first time, Susie initiated open succession conversations with one of her siblings about the future of the family-led company. In a family

where transitions often had been abrupt or secretive, this was a major shift. Choosing transparency over tradition required bravery, but it also laid the groundwork for a healthier, more sustainable legacy.

3. **Setting Boundaries**: One of Susie's boldest moves came in an important conversation she had with her father, the company's previous president. Susie prepared intentionally, set a clear boundary, and asked him to listen fully before responding. This purposeful approach changed the tone entirely, creating space for them to communicate without conflict or escalation.

Each of these moments shows what Brave Decisions look like in the real world: not loud, flashy declarations, but steady, values-focused choices made from truth. Through this process, Susie not only made better decisions, but also became a more grounded, courageous leader. She moved out of overanalysis and into aligned action. She modeled for her family and her three-hundred-employee team what it means to lead with clarity, integrity, and trust. Most importantly, she began living and leading from the Ridgewalk—not stuck in fear, not striving for approval, but instead making braver leadership decisions rooted in self-trust.

## Key Takeaways from Susie's Story:

- Investing in yourself is a leadership act: Choosing coaching defied family norms and set a new precedent for both Susie and her team.
- Transparency can be transformative: Initiating succession conversations, though risky, aligned with Susie's deeper values and created space for healthy transition.

- Strategic restructuring can serve everyone: By approaching change with determination and care, Susie made decisions that honored both business needs and human dignity.
- Energy flows from integrity: As Susie connected her actions to her deeper knowing, her confidence and impact grew.

## TRANSFORMATION BEGINS WITH THE RIDGEWALK

Brave Decisions are more than forks in the road. They are acts of alignment—moments when self-trust wins out over fear and clarity takes precedence over the status quo. Whether it was Stef reclaiming her authority as a business leader, Katie hiring from a place of vision rather than paralysis, Nadine and I investing in what we truly wanted despite temporary financial strain, or Susie restructuring her team while honoring her family's legacy, each story in this chapter reveals a different version of the same truth: Indecision and self-doubt may be familiar, but they are not where transformation lives.

True transformation begins with the Ridgewalk. As a decision-making process, the Ridgewalk doesn't eliminate fear entirely. Instead, it creates a sturdy, repeatable path through it. By guiding leaders to reconnect with their Wild Wisdom, make Brave Decisions, and have Courageous Conversations, it turns what once felt risky into what now feels right. It ensures that the bold moves you make aren't reactive or performative but rooted in integrity and possibility.

Brave Decisions are not just one-time events. They are a way of leading and living that transforms both the decision-maker and the world they influence. With every aligned choice, you reinforce a new identity: one grounded in clarity, capable of navigating uncertainty and the will to walk the risky but daring path toward Impossible Freedom when you feel fully lit up in business and life—*and* drive more financial growth at the same time.

So, if you find yourself standing at a decision point—stuck, scared, or swirling—remember that your Wild Wisdom already knows the way. The Ridgewalk is there to support you. And your next Brave Decision may be the one that changes everything.

# YOUR REFLECT TO RISE JOURNAL

**Brave Decisions in Motion:** Which of the stories in this chapter resonated most with your own experience? What made it relatable, and what did it teach you about your own decision-making patterns?

**Fear vs. Self-Trust:** Where in your life or business are you currently facing a decision clouded by fear, uncertainty, or pressure? What would change if you made the choice from self-trust and possibility instead?

**The Ridgewalk:** This chapter outlines a three-stage process for bold, aligned decision-making: Reconnect with your Wild Wisdom, make a Brave Decision, and communicate it with courage. Which step do you find most challenging and why?

**Letting Go of Trade-Offs:** The story of Nadine and Derek investing in what they each wanted at a specific moment in time challenges the belief that growth always requires sacrifice. Where in your business and life are you assuming an either/or choice when a both/and might be possible?

**Taking Action:** What Brave Decision have you been postponing? What's one small step you can take this week to move out of indecision and into aligned action?

**Community Connection:** Who in your business or life could benefit from hearing that Brave Decisions are not about recklessness or limitation, but about clarity and alignment? How might you support them through their next Ridgewalk moment?

Get the free book companion with all
reflection questions and exercises at
ascendleadership.com/book.

# COURAGEOUS CONVERSATIONS: THE POWER OF CONNECTION

*By Nadine Nicholson*

When I was in my mid-thirties, my dad's decline from stomach cancer was fast and unforgiving. During this heartbreaking time, I was fortunate to have the support of a wonderful coach, Jane, who had deep wisdom in grief, death, and the importance of saying what needs to be said. I truly believe I manifested Jane's support for this specific time in my life. She guided and encouraged me to openly share my thoughts and feelings with my dad before he passed, emphasizing the importance of not having any regrets or unsaid words later. This advice proved invaluable as his final days unfolded.

Forty-eight hours before Dad was moved into palliative care in hospital, he was at home in bed. He and my mom lived an hour away from me and Derek. It was a sweltering holiday weekend in August, and I spent as much time with them as possible. Having begun to experience more and more pain, Dad slept a lot. I tried to find a moment when he was awake and cognizant, hoping to have a meaningful conversation with him. The opportunity never came; he was too tired or incoherent to talk.

On Monday afternoon, almost overcome with disappointment, I went home. That evening, Mom called me. "You may want to come back," she said gently. "I think there may be a good window after he wakes up."

I immediately jumped in the car and drove the hour back. Sure enough, there was about a thirty-minute period when Dad opened his eyes, and I could see the real him staring back at me. He was himself. He was present.

I sat on the carpet beside his bed, took his hand, and asked if I could share a few things with him. He nodded yes.

What followed was one of the most sacred and courageous conversations of my life. I told him how proud I was to be his daughter. I told him about my memory of him teaching me how to skate and ride a bike. He became emotional and proud. Later, he rightly pointed out that many of my friends' dads chose to spend their time out at the bar instead of at home with their kids. But not him. We talked about camping and growing up on an acreage and what a beautiful gift he'd given me by connecting me so deeply with Mother Nature. He'd also helped me get a good education, put a roof over my head, gave me the opportunity to travel across Canada and the United States, and taught me about real estate.

I shared that I dreamed of living by a lake or river one day. He encouraged me. "Go for it. Make sure you and Derek do it together." He said, "I want to tell you something. Marriage isn't all roses, but make sure you don't bicker with each other."

I told Dad we wanted a second child (which would never come to pass), and he encouraged me not to wait too long. Dad also made me promise to take care of Mom after he was gone. "If you get any sniff of someone taking advantage of her," he whispered, "get on it and take care of it."

As our conversation began to wind down, Dad said he was glad I'd had a chance to share everything I'd wanted to. "How long do you think I have left?" he asked.

"I'm not sure," I answered honestly, tears in my eyes. "You seem to be getting weaker."

"I think I've got four weeks," he said.

He only had four days.

This final exchange, facilitated by the wisdom of my coach and my mom's intuition, remains one of the most courageous and vulnerable moments of connection I've ever experienced. Not because it was eloquent or tidy, but because it was honest. It was present. It was human. There was no performance, no perfection, no attempt to control the outcome. Just love, truth, and a willingness to say what mattered most.

That's what this chapter is about. Courageous Conversations are not just about giving feedback or setting boundaries at work. They're not just business tools. They're the foundation of strong leadership because they're the foundation of meaningful relationships. They are what make us human. They require bravery. Kindness. Firmness. Vulnerability. Clarity. Compassion. Above all, they demand a commitment to truth in service of connection.

In the pages that follow, we'll explore what Courageous Conversations look like in leadership, business, and life, and how they help you protect your time, lead your team, serve your clients, and achieve Impossible Freedom. You'll hear stories from leaders who chose to speak up rather than stay silent, even when it was uncomfortable. You'll learn the patterns that keep so many high performers stuck in avoidance and the practical tools that help shift fear into clarity. And you'll discover that the conversations we avoid cost us more than we realize. The conversations we have the courage to have open the door to everything that matters.

## THE COURAGEOUS CONVERSATIONS THAT CHANGE EVERYTHING

Courageous Conversations are the third and final Leadership Amplifier in the Impossible Freedom Equation. If Wild Wisdom helps you hear your inner truth, and Brave Decisions help you act on it, then Courageous Conversations are how you voice it. Through intentional dialogue and genuine connection, you begin to shape your external world in alignment with your internal clarity. At its core, a Courageous Conversation is the act of speaking your ideas, needs, desires, and boundaries with clarity and conviction.

Courageous Conversations often arise at pivotal moments in life and business, when you're called to take action and navigate relationships despite fear, uncertainty, or discomfort. These conversations typically aren't loud or dramatic. More often they are quiet and focused, marked by honesty, directness, and respect. Whether you're speaking with a client, potential client, team member, supplier, banker, or a loved one, the purpose remains the same: to create connection through truth, not control.

You'll often sense when a Courageous Conversation is needed—not with logic, but in your body. You'll feel a tightening in your shoulders. A nervous flutter in your stomach. A recurring thought you try to deny or push from your mind.

These physical cues are your internal compass, letting you know the moment matters. Courageous Conversations tend to be the ones you avoid, replay in your head, or silently dread. Yet putting them off only increases emotional pressure and deepens fear. When you choose to speak up with kindness and firmness, you create space for resolution, reciprocity, and a palpable sense of relief.

Before working with us, many of our clients delay or avoid these conversations for weeks or even months, only to say afterward, "Why didn't I do that sooner?" Often the imagined worst-case scenario is far more distressing than the reality. When guided by intention, the simple act of naming what's true becomes a powerful leadership practice. The conversation itself may be uncomfortable, but the outcome is usually far more constructive and freeing than anticipated.

This Leadership Amplifier is about more than improving your communication skills. Courageous Conversations prevent energy leaks caused by avoidance, guessing, or unresolved tension. They reduce mental clutter by clarifying expectations and boundaries. They restore agency by giving you a voice in the moments, big and small, that shape the direction of your life. And they cultivate trust through sincerity, empathy, and respect.

In both work and life, Courageous Conversations are foundational to effective leadership. They shift you from reactive to responsive, from misalignment to clarity. Your team becomes more self-reliant. Your clients feel genuinely seen and supported. You spend less time managing misunderstandings and more time creating what matters. In your personal life, relationships with partners, children, family, and friends become richer as communication strengthens. Silence is no longer the default response to discomfort. Instead, connection grows through shared understanding.

Anne of Sagent experienced this firsthand. For years she had been part of a women CEOs mastermind group that energized and inspired her, but something shifted after speaking with Nadine. She could see the vision for a new way forward working fewer hours in her business. Anne struggled with how she could continue to get advice from the mastermind group *and* embark on a whole new direction to achieve the vision for her personal and professional life that she co-designed with Nadine.

During our work together, Anne gained a new level of clarity: Just because something *once* supported her doesn't mean it is aligned with who she is *today*. She realized that continuing to pour her limited time and energy into a space that no longer reflected her current goals was holding her back. Rather than quietly pull away or make excuses, Anne chose to have an honest, in-person conversation with the women she had grown alongside. It wasn't easy for her. She feared disappointing them and worried about being misunderstood, but she also knew that staying silent would cost her more than temporary discomfort ever could.

Anne shared her Brave Decision to leave the mastermind group with kindness and simplicity, expressing that while she was grateful for her peers' support, her business and personal growth had moved in a new direction. To her surprise, the group responded not with judgment, but with encouragement. Anne's willingness to communicate openly and honestly gave others permission to reflect on their own needs. What could have been a moment of separation became a moment of deeper connection for everyone involved.

This is the power of Courageous Conversations. They don't just shift what's happening between people; they shift what's possible. It's not about confrontation. It's about connection through truth-telling. When done with care and intention, these conversations foster alignment, inspire clarity, and model a more human, heart-centered way of leading.

And the rewards are significant. When Courageous Conversations become part of how you live and lead, you experience less tension and more ease. You spend less time reacting and more time creating. You move past unnecessary drama and toward genuine alignment. Most of all, you cultivate more peace, both in your relationships and within yourself. This is what Impossible Freedom feels like: not fewer responsibilities but fewer regrets; not a lighter workload but clearer focus; not only more success but also true satisfaction. Every time you choose to have a Courageous Conversation, that's what it delivers.

## THE COST OF STAYING SILENT AND LOSING REAL-TIME CONNECTION

Few things are more costly in leadership than silence rooted in fear and avoidance. It doesn't preserve relationships; it strains them. It doesn't cultivate trust; it erodes it. Instead of moving your business forward, silence keeps progress just out of reach. Every avoided conversation comes with a cost. This cost isn't always visible at first. It accumulates through misunderstood expectations, missed opportunities, delayed decisions, duplicated work, wasted time, and lingering tension. It depletes your energy, weakens your relationships, and diminishes your leadership potential.

Silence may feel like a shortcut to safety, but it creates space for assumptions, resentment, and the anxious energy that grows in the absence of truth and honesty. While avoidance can give the illusion of harmony, it also creates confusion and erodes confidence over time. The longer you wait, the heavier the emotional burden becomes. Like standing at the edge of a zip line platform, hesitation makes the leap feel more terrifying. Your mind spins worst-case scenarios. Your body reacts physically. Your inner storyteller fills in the blanks, usually with fear.

Technology amplifies the cost of silence. When we hide behind tools like email and text messages, we avoid the vulnerability and grace of a real-time human connection. Asynchronous communication may feel more efficient, but it often slows decisions and drains emotional energy. You send a message and wait. Wonder. Second-guess. You try to interpret tone and intention through text, sometimes spinning stories in your head about what the other person is thinking. This is where meaning gets lost and anxiety takes hold.

Courageous Conversations rely on synchronous communication when two or more people interact with each other in real time, either in person or remotely. This involves direct conversation with immediate feedback and no lag time. Some examples are in-person meetings, phone or video calls, and live webinars or classes. The benefits of synchronous communication include faster decision-making, improved team alignment, stronger relationship building, increased creativity, and immediate conflict resolution. This is best used for time-sensitive issues, complex, high-stakes negotiations, or sensitive, emotional conversations.

In contrast, asynchronous communication refers to any kind of communication when a delay occurs between the time a message is sent and the time the person on the other end receives and interprets it. Some examples are emails, voicemails, text messages, recorded messages, project management tools (Asana, Jira, Slack/Teams messages), Loom videos, and shared documents.

The benefits of asynchronous communication include flexibility in response time and better documentation. This is best used for non-urgent updates, detailed feedback, status reports, and brainstorming that doesn't need immediate resolution.

Many people overuse asynchronous communication tools to create a paper trail, avoid perceived conflict, and avoid direct contact with people. But communicating asynchronously can hinder connection between people and foster misunderstandings, worry, faulty assumptions, and loss of opportunity to improve relationships. Worst-case scenarios and negative meaning-making fester in the silences between sent and received messages. Ironically, rather than save you time, asynchronous communication leaks a massive amount of your time and energy because it can create worry, over-thinking, and a false sense of safety and control. Currently, as technology has increased, much of our society is afraid of synchronous communication. We've become less and less accustomed to it, so we resist it.

This idea isn't new. I learned it back in 1999 when completing my Bachelor of Communications in Public Relations degree. In an article for the *Harvard Business Review*, psychiatrist Edward M. Hallowell explores how authentic face-to-face interactions or "human moments" in modern workplaces are increasingly dominated by digital communication.[3] He explains that for a genuine human moment to take place, two key components are required: physical presence and focused attention. These moments strengthen trust, understanding, and creativity. Positive in-person contact triggers the release of hormones like oxytocin, which also nurtures trust and

---

[3] Edward M. Hallowell, "The Human Moment at Work," *Harvard Business Review* 77, no. 1 (January–February 1998): 58–66.

reduces stress. Virtual interactions fail to replicate this effect, and the rise of digital tools have led to miscommunication, alienation, and "toxic worry," or anxiety caused by ambiguous or impersonal electronic interactions.

Hallowell wrote this article in 1998, before the internet became what it is today, before smartphones, social media, cloud-based team communication platforms, ChatGPT, and other generative AI tools. Yet since then, nothing has changed about the role synchronous communication plays in our success. It's how humans thrive. It always has been. Technology will never be an effective substitute for the depth and value of human connection.

Consider how Stef came to work with us at Ascend Leadership Co. After hearing me speak at a conference in Phoenix, Arizona, she expressed interest in joining our former group coaching program, which was our entry level offering at the time. But through further conversations with her, I knew it wasn't the right fit. What Stef truly needed was private, personalized executive leadership coaching. That offering came with a higher price tag. Proposing it could be seen as risky since it wasn't what she had in mind. I could have gone for the easier sale, but I didn't. I chose to have a Courageous Conversation.

"Can I share what's coming up for me?" I asked.

"Go for it," Stef replied.

I told her why personalized executive leadership coaching was the best way to achieve the transformation she was seeking. Selling her a group program just because it was an easy sale wouldn't serve her. I showed up in full service of her and spoke the higher truth, even if it risked her walking away.

Stef enrolled in private coaching with me and Derek, and she's thanked us ever since. "I am so beyond grateful to have the two of you in my corner, on my team. Thank you so much for the authentic and inspiring way you guide me toward the next version of myself in all facets of my business and life," she told us later. "I'm your biggest fan and so thankful I met Nadine at the conference in Phoenix, making one of my most important connections ever." The Courageous Conversation we had deepened our relationship and set the tone for the work we'd do together.

Courageous Conversations are more than business tools. They are a philosophy of presence. A way of honoring what you see, feel, and know—and sharing it for both your own benefit and the benefit to others. In leadership, that means offering your clearest insight with kindness and firmness, even when it's edgy, uncomfortable, and inconvenient. Over the years, I've had countless Courageous Conversations with clients, partners, family members, friends, Uber drivers, and others all around the world. When I reflect on the most meaningful moments, they weren't in formal meetings or milestone presentations. They were in shared stories with a client over tapas in Pennsylvania, laughter with a client's child by a river in Virginia, or a quiet heart-to-heart with a client over sushi in California. Each of these moments had one thing in common: presence. Authentic, open, human connection.

Every relationship offers a choice. You can either stay surface-level and safe or go deeper and build something lasting. Courageous Conversations are how you choose depth. They are the bridge between knowing what matters and letting others in on it. So, if you've been feeling disconnected from your team, unclear with your clients, distant in your relationships, or exhausted from the guessing games silence creates, start here. Have the conversation. Pick up the phone instead of sending an email. Ask the question you've been avoiding.

Say the thing that's true and hard and generous. Because the cost of silence is too high, and the reward of connection is too great to miss.

## TOOLS AND TECHNIQUES FOR PRACTICING COURAGEOUS CONVERSATIONS

Courageous Conversations don't require perfection. They require intention. One of the most powerful ways to ground your message and show up with clarity and care is to use proven communication tools and techniques that help you stay present. One of the most powerful tools I use personally and professionally is called the CAP Framework. CAP stands for concern, action, and perspective. It's simple. It's flexible. And it works in almost every context, whether I'm speaking with my team, a coaching client, a supplier, my husband, or my son.

I first learned this framework during one of the most high-stakes chapters of my corporate career. At the time, I was the issues management and crisis communications manager for a $3 billion energy company publicly traded on the New York and Toronto Stock Exchanges. I was responsible for reputation management, crisis communications, and media relations, which meant I often helped the CEO and CFO navigate highly sensitive situations in the public eye.

One day we faced a serious crisis: An employee had made an internal error that eventually cost the company $33 million. I don't use the word "crisis" lightly. This was a publicly traded company; a mistake of that magnitude could tank investor confidence and trigger a significant drop in our stock price.

In situations like this, you have a choice: You can hide behind technicalities and wait for the minimum investor disclosure window, or you can lead with transparency and honesty and own the message. We chose the latter, and I leveraged my CAP Framework to shape our CEO's messaging to clearly explain the issue to the company's key internal and external audiences, including the senior executive team, employees, shareholders, and the media. Here's what that looked like:

1. **Concern:** Our CEO acknowledged the issue openly and directly, disclosing it a full month before he was technically required to, and he was explicit about that choice. He explained what had happened, why it mattered, and why we were taking it seriously. Taking responsibility, he defined and problem and expressed regret without spin or deflection—just honesty.
2. **Action:** Next, the CEO outlined the specific steps we had already taken to investigate, contain, and resolve the error.
3. **Perspective:** Finally, he showed what the issue meant in the greater sense, putting the issue into perspective. He shared what was being done to prevent this issue from happening again and to mitigate any further impact. He offered a clear and confident view of what stakeholders could expect moving forward, including our strategy, next milestones, and ongoing commitment to transparency.

What happened next was remarkable. Yes, our stock price fell in the first few days after the announcement, creating that initial loss of $33 million. By the seven-day mark, however, our stock price had not only recovered, but it also climbed higher than it was before the incident. Investors and the media rewarded us for our accountability and forthright leadership. We didn't only protect our reputation; we strengthened it.

This experience taught me the lifelong value of my CAP Framework in guiding Courageous Conversations. Here's how to use it:

1. **Concern:** Start by naming the issue and explaining why it matters. This creates shared context.

   "Here's the situation, and here's why I care about it . . ."
2. **Action:** Describe the steps you've taken to manage the issue or decisions you've made so far. This builds credibility and shows responsibility.

   "Here's what I've done already to address it . . ."
3. **Perspective:** This is all about what the issue means in the greater sense. Share what you're thinking about next, what others can expect, or where you plan to go from here. This provides reassurance and direction.

   "Here's what I see coming next, and here's what I'd like your input on . . ."

   To make your conversations even more collaborative, add a fourth step:
4. **Like Best, Next Time (LB/NT):** After you've shared your message, invite the other person or people to reflect with you by asking: "What did you like best about this situation/decision/approach?" and "What would you suggest for next time?" LB/NT turns your message into a dialogue. It helps close the loop, keeps feedback flowing, and builds stronger relationships. It's one of my favorite ways to model curiosity and continuous improvement.

Alongside the CAP Framework, I consistently rely on a set of strategic communication techniques, both in my own life and when guiding our executive leadership coaching clients, to navigate meaningful or pivotal conversations. These are especially helpful when emotions are high, the stakes are personal, or fear and vulnerability are getting in the way of action.

1. **Pause, Notice, and Name Your Fear:** When you find yourself avoiding a conversation, take a moment to pause. Breathe. Reconnect with your intention. Ask yourself: "What's the real issue here? What are the facts? What meaning and stories am I making up about this interaction?" Fear thrives in silence and urgency. But when you slow down enough to observe the fear, name it, and separate it from the facts, it loses its grip. This is the first step to reclaiming your agency, and it connects to the Ridgewalk we discussed in Chapter 5. To notice your fear and break its hold, first you have to stop walking along the ridge. By pausing, you're better able to see fear not as an enemy to conquer, but as a signal pointing to what matters most.

2. **Access Your Wild Wisdom:** Most people already know what they need to say, but fear and overthinking cloud the message. By shifting from the head to the heart and gut, you tap into your Wild Wisdom. Ask yourself: "If I strip away my fear, if I breathe deeply, if I plant my feet on the earth, what do I believe? What am I feeling and seeing and hearing? What do I want to say, really?"

3. **Lead with Values:** Instead of speaking from urgency or pressure, root your message in something more profound (integrity, care, respect, shared purpose). This makes the conversation intentional instead of reactive. When others understand the purpose behind your words, they're more likely to stay open and connected.

4. **Role-play and Meaning-Making:** Think through how you want the conversation to go (for example, identifying key messages with the CAP Framework), then role-play with

someone you trust. With our clients, we reflect their language back to them, acknowledging what works and what can be elevated or more aligned. It's about helping you find words that are both true and effective, transforming your worst-case scenarios into best-case scenarios, and manifesting them through positive rather than negative meaning-making.

5. **Prepare to be Present:** While role-play can be very useful, don't over-script every Courageous Conversation. It's more important to get clear about what matters most and stay grounded. This allows you to show up with calm clarity, not pressure and control. It's about being present and responsive, not rehearsed.

6. **Develop Empathy:** Do the difficult work of trying to understand the possible fears, motivations, needs, and emotional state of whom you're speaking to. This changes the relationship dynamic from "opponents" to "partners." It's not just about what you say, but how you anticipate and react to what's heard. Empathy allows you to create real two-way dialogue, creating curiosity and compassion that leads to strong relationship-building.

7. **Anchor in Growth and Self-Trust:** Before a Courageous Conversation, ground yourself in who you are and the kind of leader you're becoming—not to be perfect but to lead with integrity. Remember a time you spoke your truth. Then let that remind you of your strength and ability to do difficult things. After the conversation, pause to reflect. Whether through journaling or debriefing with a trusted advisor, use each experience to build self-trust, clarity, and confidence. Courageous Conversations are a leadership practice, and each one strengthens your ability to face the next.

Together these communication techniques transform Courageous Conversations from something scary into something deeply empowering. They don't make the conversation easy, but they do make it more impactful. They help you move from avoidance to aligned action, from fear to truth. They create more human, honest, and connected interactions. Over time what once felt daunting becomes a core leadership skill you can rely on, and if they helped me navigate a $33 million crisis, they can help you too.

## FROM AVOIDANCE TO AUTHENTICITY IN ONE SENTENCE

When Susie first came to us, she was already a respected and successful leader. As president of a family-owned business, Susie carried the weight of legacy, culture, and team well-being. But like so many high-performing leaders, she also carried something less visible: an unhealthy habit of avoiding high-stakes conversations. Despite her warmth and presence, Susie often delayed difficult conversations out of fear. She was afraid of being misunderstood, saying the wrong thing, and damaging important relationships. Ironically, in trying to protect those relationships, she unintentionally weakened them. The result? Misunderstandings festered. Stress mounted. Decisions stalled. And the emotional labor of holding it all together while appearing composed depleted her.

This pattern began to shift through coaching with me and Derek. Susie began to see that communicating with courage isn't about controlling the outcome; it's about moving forward with truth, clarity, and values. She learned to separate facts from fear-based narratives, to recognize when she was over-functioning, and to speak with calm conviction rather than anxious over-explanation. What once felt overwhelming began to feel empowering.

In Chapter 4, we first mentioned one of Susie's pivotal Courageous Conversations: a boundary-setting interaction with her father. In this chapter, we take a closer look at what made that moment so transformational.

Susie's father is highly respected and has long been a guiding force in their family and business. Their previous attempts at sensitive conversations often ended in frustration. "My dad tends to listen to respond, not to understand," Susie explained. "In the past, I'd try to express something important, and it would turn into a circular, exhausting loop."

This time Susie tried something new. She used the leadership practices we taught her to get grounded and centered beforehand, and when the conversation began, she set a kind but firm boundary. "Here's what I'm going to talk about," she told him, "and I really need you to just listen until I'm finished."

It was a single sentence, but it changed everything.

Setting this small but powerful boundary flipped the entire tone of the conversation. Her father listened fully. Susie spoke clearly and confidently. What had once been a dreaded interaction became productive, respectful, and connective.

"It seems so obvious in hindsight," she reflected later, "but that opening completely changed how my dad received what I had to say."

This was more than a communication win. It was a moment of leadership. Susie found her voice and used it to reshape the dynamics around her, without needing to dominate or diminish others in the process. From that moment forward, something clicked. Susie began having conversations she'd long avoided with her team, other family members, and even herself. She no longer felt the need to have everything perfectly planned before speaking up. She embraced messiness. She trusted her intuition. Most of all, she started showing up with greater authenticity and less performance.

"I was amazed at how well these conversations went once I actually had them," she shared. "The relief was incredible. Learning to be true to myself and not trying to be someone I'm not has completely changed how I lead."

We can all learn from Susie. Her growth shows that when you stop performing and start expressing what's real, what you actually need, and what you actually think, you create the conditions for deeper trust, both around you and within you. In that space of honesty, leadership becomes a force for alignment, courage, and meaningful change, and that's when leadership stops being a role you play and starts becoming who you are.

## PRACTICING THE COURAGE TO CONNECT

Courageous Conversations are not just a communication skill. They're a leadership practice, a relational practice, and a freedom practice. They bridge the space between what you know is true, what you most need to say, and what the people around you most need to hear. In the end, real transformation happens in real time, in the moments when you stop spinning stories and start speaking with clarity and care.

At Ascend Leadership Co. this is the work we do every day. Every executive leadership coaching session is a Courageous Conversation. Not because they are all high stakes, but because they make visible what so often gets ignored: the blind spots, the stuck patterns, the inner noise that holds leaders back. Most leaders don't come to us lacking ability. They come to us weighed down by a fear of being misunderstood, worry about damaging a relationship, or pressure to get the words exactly right. In that hesitation, emotional pressure builds. Silence takes hold. And what could be resolved in five minutes becomes a source of ongoing stress, disconnection, or delay.

Courageous Conversations begin not with a script but with a feeling. A knot in your stomach. A recurring thought you can't shake. Lost sleep. A moment when staying silent starts to feel more painful than speaking up. That's when change can begin. From there, we help leaders pause and tell the difference between what's real and what fear is conjuring. We guide them to access their Wild Wisdom, the deeper clarity that already knows what needs to be said. Then, together, we shape it into language that feels clear, kind, and aligned. We rehearse, refine, and reflect. Once they have the conversation, we help integrate what shifted as a result. Growth doesn't end when the words are spoken; it unfolds in the experience that follows.

These conversations are not limited to offices. They happen in homes, hallways, and hospital rooms. They unfold between colleagues, co-founders, partners, and parents. They aren't about finding the perfect words. They're about showing up with honesty, intention, and respect. When Susie asked her father to listen without interruption, she wasn't only changing a conversation. She was changing a lifelong dynamic. When I chose honesty over the easy sale with Stef, we built long-term trust and an amazing working relationship. When Anne shared her Brave Decision to leave a longtime mastermind group, she gave others permission to reflect on their own needs. When I faced a $33 million corporate crisis, it was courage, not polish, that propelled the company forward. And when I sat beside my dad's bed in his final days, I learned the most sacred conversations are often the simplest ones.

That's the heart of Courageous Conversations. They interrupt cycles of avoidance, fear, and anxiety. They strip away performance and replace it with presence. They don't just restore trust with others; they build trust within yourself. They are how we lead with truth, how we build teams that thrive, and how we protect what matters most. If you've been waiting for the perfect words, the ideal timing, or the guarantee of a happy ending, don't. Start with what's true. Say what needs to be said, even if your voice shakes. Be willing to go first.

You may not be able to control the outcome, but you can lead the moment. And often that's more than enough to change everything.

# YOUR REFLECT TO RISE JOURNAL

**The Cost of Silence:** Where in your life or business are you currently paying the cost of silence? What is it costing you in energy, clarity, or connection?

**Moments That Matter:** Think of a conversation you've had, or avoided, that changed the course of a relationship. What made it courageous? What relationships in your life are calling for a more open, present, or even sacred dialogue?

**Signs and Signals:** This chapter shows that Courageous Conversations often begin with a feeling. When was the last time you had that gut-level knowing that something, perhaps something you were avoiding, had to be said? How does your body typically signal that a Courageous Conversation is needed? What patterns, physical or emotional, do you notice?

**Practicing with Intention:** What tools or techniques from this chapter resonate with you the most? How might you experiment with one of them this week?

**From Avoidance to Authenticity:** Susie's story shows that one sentence can change the tone of an entire relationship. What's one phrase or message you've been holding back that might create clarity or healing? What would change in your leadership if you replaced emotional performance with emotional presence?

**Taking Action:** What conversation have you been avoiding? What's one thing you can do this week to prepare for it, begin it, or move closer to having it with clarity and care?

**Community Connection:** What aspect of Courageous Conversations would be meaningful to share with someone else in your life or business? Whom do you know who might benefit from hearing that hard conversations can be a gift, not a threat?

PART 3

# EXPERIENCE IMPOSSIBLE FREEDOM

# CRAFTING *YOUR* VISION OF IMPOSSIBLE FREEDOM: ASCENDED POSSIBILITY AND SELF-LEADERSHIP

*By Nadine Nicholson*

I'm excited you've reached the third and final part of our journey together. If you've made it this far, you've already done some of the hardest work. You've confronted the cost of the Middle Zone and explored the full Impossible Freedom Equation, including two foundational Leadership Pillars and three powerful Amplifiers. You've learned to identify the Say/ Do and Support Gaps that quietly drain your time and erode your energy. You've loosened your grip on overwork and overthinking. You've experimented with new ways of leading your team. You've created space in your days for what truly matters, listening to your instincts and speaking your truth. And through it all, you've begun to glimpse an easier and more fulfilling path, one where you can live your best life and grow your business without the trade-offs.

The shifts you've uncovered in these pages aren't surface-level adjustments; they're evidence of a deeper transformation already underway. After all, you wouldn't have been drawn to this book if something in you wasn't ready for change. And now, as you begin to step into that change, you may feel like you're standing at the edge of something larger. But change doesn't happen all at once. The old patterns haven't completely fallen away. The world around you hasn't changed overnight; it's still full of deadlines, decisions, and team dynamics that need navigating. In fact, the pull of old patterns might feel louder than ever, especially now that you're aware of them and actively working to leave them behind. This is one of the most pivotal points on the journey. It's where many leaders begin to plateau, question their progress, or even slip back into familiar but outdated and unhelpful habits. But it's essential to know that what you're feeling isn't failure; it's friction. A natural tension between the version of you that survived the Middle Zone and the version of you now ready to live, succeed, and grow beyond it.

To move forward, you need more than systems and strategies. You need an internal compass that helps you trust what you're building, even before the results are fully visible. In this chapter, we'll explore the mindset that makes Impossible Freedom not just imaginable but achievable. We call it Ascended Possibility. It's a way of thinking that helps you lead from vision: a crisp, grounded picture of the life and business you want, rooted in purpose and available now, not someday. It's what empowers you to make aligned decisions in the face of fear and keep showing up from your truth rather than your subconscious conditioning.

You'll also meet the most important leader in your business and life: yourself. The most powerful growth you can create doesn't come from doing more but from leading yourself with clarity, trust, and integrity. That's self-leadership. When paired with Ascended Possibility, it becomes the foundation for a way of living and leading that's fully your own. This chapter concludes with an activity to help you envision what Impossible Freedom means to you and what it would look and feel like to finally escape the Middle Zone.

## ASCENDED POSSIBILITY: THE MINDSET YOU NEED TO ACHIEVE IMPOSSIBLE FREEDOM

Many high-achieving leaders stall in the Middle Zone because they keep making decisions from the same mindset that built their early success—a mindset shaped by urgency, obligation, and the fear of falling behind. Even as they long for more ease, space, and alignment, they stay trapped in familiar patterns: overcommitting, overworking, overthinking, and shrinking their vision to fit what feels safe or manageable. The result is a relentless grind where effort stays high, but fulfillment remains out of reach.

To truly move beyond the Middle Zone's limits, no hack or tactic will cut it. What you need is a new way of thinking that breaks the cycle of reactivity and makes space for real transformation. Ascended Possibility offers exactly that: a conscious elevation in how you perceive and navigate choice, decision-making, and uncertainty. It moves you out of survival mode and into creativity, opportunity, and choice.

This shift unlocks momentum that's rooted in clarity and self-trust. If you look back on Parts 1–2 of this book, you'll notice Ascended Possibility has been quietly at work all along, guiding you to meet challenges and turning points not with constraint but with conviction that something better is always available to you. Table 2 illustrates what this shift looks like in action.

**Table 2.** The Difference Between Middle Zone and Ascended Possibility Thinking—Time Mastery and United Team.

| Middle Zone Thinking | Ascended Possibility Thinking |
|---|---|
| **Time Mastery** | |
| A long to-do list is what's stressing me out. | Being out of integrity and alignment with my values is what's really causing my stress. |
| It's what I do that matters. | It's who I'm being that matters. |
| I can't do it all. | I can do all that matters and not everything matters. |
| There are right and wrong decisions. | The same decision can have different outcomes depending on whether you make that decision from the energy of self-trust or fear. |
| Impossible Freedom is impossible. I can never have this. This is for other people, not me. | Impossible Freedom is absolutely possible. This is for me too. I get to have this and can use my Impossible Freedom Equation to get there. |
| **United Team** | |
| My team consists of people I pay to work for me. | My team consists of my entire support structure. It's my employees and partners, as well as my family, friends, clients, community, and others who help me lead. |

*(Continued)*

**Table 2.** (*Continued*)

| Middle Zone Thinking | Ascended Possibility Thinking |
| --- | --- |
| Asking is selfish or weak. | I should proactively and confidently ask for help. Being supported shows strength. |
| I need to focus on efficiently managing tasks and projects. | I need to focus on effectively leading and trusting myself and my team. |

Middle Zone thinking is reactive. It's driven by fear, people-pleasing, perfectionism, and a constant sense of falling short or needing to prove your worth. Ascended Possibility thinking is expansive. It's driven by alignment, self-trust, confidence, and a willingness to make decisions based on where you want to be, not only where you are. One of our clients in Michigan illustrates this mindset well: When she led an eight-figure government contracting company, we helped her to purposefully make Brave Decisions from the perspective of a nine-figure company, since that was her revenue growth goal. She aligned her choices, investments, and strategies with the identity and operations of where she wanted to take her company, not where they currently stood. That's Ascended Possibility in action.

Another real-world application of Ascended Possibility thinking shows up in how Derek and I (and our clients) approach sales and contract negotiations. Traditional selling often comes with high pressure. Many entrepreneurs and business leaders believe the sales process is a necessary evil, something to get through quickly so you can get back to the "real" work. That way of thinking comes from unhelpful Middle Zone conditioning.

From an Ascended Possibility lens, sales and contract negotiations are simply the first act of service. It's a space to show up in full integrity, to create mutual clarity, to serve boldly whether your prospective client says yes or no. The power isn't one-sided; it's shared. In a sense, you're hiring each other. Empowered Sales means both parties are empowered in the negotiation. There is reciprocity. The goal isn't to close but to connect. When you think from a place of Ascended Possibility, you stop hustling for the yes. You stop trying to be persuasive. Instead, you lead the conversation from value and integrity. You recognize that the return on your prospective client's time begins the moment they enter a conversation with you. The result? You start attracting more of the right clients, doing less convincing and pushing, and building longer-lasting, more easeful relationships. Table 3 demonstrates how this shift fosters empowered sales.

When you think and act from the elevated perspective of Ascended Possibility, your approach to selling and contract

**Table 3.** The Difference Between Middle Zone and Ascended Possibility Thinking—Empowered Sales.

| Middle Zone Thinking | Ascended Possibility Thinking |
|---|---|
| **Empowered Sales and Contract Negotiations** ||
| The sales process is uncomfortable and one-sided. | Sales is a co-creation and values-aligned dialogue. |
| Always be selling. | Always be serving. |
| Automate and funnel prospective clients. | Prioritize real relationships and direct connection. |
| It's about closing the deal. | It's about depth, duration, and right-fit resonance. |
| Take any clients who come through your door. | Claim and stand for your ideal, best-fit clients. |

negotiations becomes a mirror of your leadership. It reveals how you think, how deeply you trust yourself, and how you create space for clarity, connection, and mutual value. But the impact doesn't stop there. Ascended Possibility shapes how you prepare for Courageous Conversations, how you manage your time, how you relate to your team, and how you move through change. It's not a surface-level tweak. It's a shift in who you are and how you see the world, helping you resist the gravitational pull of the Middle Zone and anchor into a way of being profoundly more honest and sustainable.

Here's what defines the Ascended Possibility mindset:

- It's vision-anchored: You use the vision of Impossible Freedom as your north star, never forgetting where you should be pointed to keep making progress.
- It's elevated: You think from a future state, not from what's urgent or familiar.
- It's integrated: You bring Wild Wisdom, Brave Decisions, and Courageous Conversations into your daily actions.
- It's disruptive in the best way: It challenges outdated thinking and replaces it with choices grounded in integrity.
- It's continuous: This is not a one-time mindset shift; it's a way of thinking that becomes foundational to how you live and lead.

As leaders like you begin to adopt this mindset, the shifts you experience are often subtle but powerful. Instead of shrinking a decision to make it more manageable, you grow your capacity to hold a bigger vision. Instead of trying to fix a scheduling problem, you examine what beliefs are shaping your time in the first place. And instead of relying on conditioned logic alone, you tune into deeper sources of wisdom like intuition, self-trust, and values.

Over time these inner shifts lead to tangible change:

- You start making fewer decisions from fear and more from trust.
- You lead with clarity and conviction instead of urgency or approval-seeking.
- Your business becomes a reflection of your values, not just a container for your output.
- You hold boundaries and vision with equal strength, without apology.

One decision, one mindset shift, one aligned moment at a time—this is how Impossible Freedom stops being an abstract idea and becomes your lived experience. The path forward isn't about striving harder. It's about thinking differently, trusting more deeply, and making small, grounded choices that reflect who you're becoming.

## SELF-LEADERSHIP: THE HEART OF SUSTAINABLE BUSINESS GROWTH

At the heart of the Impossible Freedom Equation is a powerful truth: Leadership isn't a collection of tools or quick wins. It's learning to lead from your natural strengths with clarity, integrity, and intention. The journey doesn't start with team dynamics or business strategy. It starts with you. Before you can lead others effectively, you must be willing to learn to lead yourself. This is the essence of self-leadership.

Self-leadership is the daily practice of guiding your thoughts, decisions, actions, and energy from a place of inner alignment and Wild Wisdom. It's the ability to stay rooted in your values and vision, even under pressure, and to lead yourself with the same compassion and conviction you extend to others. It's not about control or perfection. It's about presence. It means making Brave Decisions and having Courageous Conversations that reflect who you are and what you truly stand for, not just what others expect. At its core, self-leadership is the foundation of sustainable and scalable growth—because you can't lead a team, a business, or a mission if you're not first willing to lead yourself.

If Impossible Freedom is the summit you're striving to reach, and Ascended Possibility is the mindset that keeps you climbing, then self-leadership is the path beneath your feet. And as with Ascended Possibility, self-leadership is quietly woven through Parts 1–2 of this book too, showing up every time Derek and I invite you to act with clarity, claim your truth, or choose alignment over obligation and limitation.

For many leaders, embracing self-leadership is a defining turning point. You may have built your success by working harder than everyone else, saying yes too often, and being constantly accessible, but it came at a steep cost: fatigue, frustration, and a growing sense of disconnection. When you begin practicing self-leadership in earnest, you realize the patterns that once sustained your success can no longer sustain your well-being. Overworking and overcommitting stop feeling noble and start feeling depleting. You begin to see that the essence of leadership isn't about managing everything; it's about anchoring yourself in what truly matters and making decisions from that deeper place of awareness and knowing.

When practiced consistently, self-leadership transforms every domain of your business and life:

- You lead your time by focusing on what's essential, rather than reacting to every urgency or expectation.
- You lead your team by modeling clarity, courage, and stability.
- You lead your decisions by trusting your own wisdom, taking brave action, and speaking truth with courage.
- You lead your life as an integrated whole, instead of splitting yourself between personal and professional roles.

Most leaders are taught to sacrifice personal time for business success and results. We're here to teach the opposite. Work-life integration, not work-life balance, is the answer to living a deeply fulfilling life while driving business growth, without compromising one for the other. You don't have to wear different hats or switch between roles. You don't need one version of yourself for work and another for home. The presence and alignment you bring to business decisions should also guide you in parenting, partnership, health, or money. Growth isn't meant to be compartmentalized. It's meant to be integrated.

The Ridgewalk decision-making process is one of the most effective tools you have to build your self-leadership. It guides you through three key steps: accessing your Wild Wisdom, making a Brave Decision, and communicating courageously about that decision. Each step is simple, but together they form a grounded self-leadership rhythm that keeps you rooted in your own truth and forward motion. What makes this so powerful is how naturally it shows up when you're leading yourself through real-life challenges. It's not just a reflection tool; it's a way of overcoming uncertainty with conviction.

One of the most profound examples of self-leadership I've experienced didn't happen in a boardroom or during a client meeting. It happened during a medical crisis on a trip with my extended family in Mexico. My eighty-two-year-old mom, Marge, had brought us all together—her daughters, sons-in-law, and grandkids—for an all-inclusive vacation at the Barceló Maya Palace resort. On the final night, after a joyful family dinner, she slipped and fell on some water in her hotel room, fracturing a vertebra in her back. What followed were five intense days of crisis management as I advocated for Mom in a foreign healthcare system, navigated language barriers, coordinated international insurance and travel arrangements, made high-stakes medical and financial decisions, supported her through emergency spinal surgery, and oversaw her journey home to Canada.

I didn't have a playbook. What I did have was presence, Ascended Possibility, self-leadership, my United Team, and the Ridgewalk. I stayed grounded and asked informed questions with kindness and firmness. I trusted medical professionals while doing my due diligence, without trying to control every detail. I leaned on the support and skills of my family, travel agent, executive assistant, and other colleagues. I led myself moment by moment through a sensitive situation that demanded emotional steadiness, aligned decision-making, and trust in me and others.

The Ridgewalk wasn't something I consciously applied; it was simply how I moved through the situation. Wild Wisdom showed up in the quiet but steady instinct I had to trust the private hospital team and move forward with the surgery, even without direct insurance billing in place. Brave Decisions were required repeatedly, from coordinating a multiple five-figure up-front payment, to navigating international logistics on little sleep, to advocating for Mom while staying clearheaded. And Courageous Conversations took many forms: voicing questions and uncertainty with doctors, sharing emotional updates with family and delegating tasks to them, and later allowing myself to be vulnerable enough to cry and receive support when it was all over.

Only after we got home safely and Mom was recovering did the emotional weight of what we'd been through hit me. I let go and broke down in tears, overcome with the pressure I'd been holding. And that moment, too, was an act of self-leadership. I let myself be supported by Derek and my sister, who reassured me: "You were the right person for this. You were made for this. You got Mom safely back home to Canada."

That experience reaffirmed what I know to be true: You don't only need self-leadership in the office. Self-leadership empowers you to be aligned in the chaos, clear in your values, willing to let others help, and integrated across your whole life. The Ridgewalk lives in these integrated moments not because you planned for it, but because you've practiced trusting yourself enough to walk it. This is exactly the kind of growth our client Susie experienced when she stopped waiting for the right conditions and started leading herself with conviction and clarity.

When she and I first met, Susie was carrying a quiet but crushing concern. "I'm really worried my leadership team is burning out," she told me, her eyes welling up as she spoke.

At first Susie thought the solution was to provide more leadership development support to her team, but as we dug deeper, something important came into view: Susie was modeling the very burnout she feared her team was experiencing. Like many leaders, she had been conditioned to believe that investing in the business and her workforce was smart. Necessary. Worthy. But investing in herself? That felt indulgent. No one had ever told her she was the number one asset in the business. That she needed to treat her own leadership development in the same way she supported her team members' development. Supporting herself wasn't selfish; it was strategic.

Through our work together, Susie began to shift from inherited expectations and obligations to embodied self-leadership. She began applying the Ridgewalk as a daily practice. She began trusting herself, tuning into her Wild Wisdom, and honoring what she knew to be true even when it was uncomfortable. She made values-based Brave Decisions despite fear. She initiated Courageous Conversations that allowed her to lead more fully. And she stopped feeling pressure to mimic the command-and-control leadership style that had been modeled for her. Instead, she chose her natural way of collaboration, ease, and presence as her leadership style.

Susie's transformation didn't happen overnight, but it was undeniable. She reclaimed her energy. She restructured how she used her time. She expanded her capacity to lead and began holding space for herself and her team in a way that didn't drain her. What makes Susie's story powerful is that she not only transformed her business, but also redefined leadership in both work and life, making self-trust and alignment the foundation of sustainable success for herself and her team.

That's the possibility self-leadership unlocks. It calls you to trust yourself, even in fear and uncertainty. To take the next step not because the path is perfect, but because your presence and perspective are strong. When you lead this way, you hold vision, boundaries, and compassion together without sacrificing any parts of yourself. This is exactly what we want for you. Not a formula. Not dependency. Instead, a way of leading that's fully your own. Because when you learn to lead yourself from the inside out, Impossible Freedom stops being something to chase. It becomes the natural expression of how you live and lead every day, feeling fully lit up in business and life—*and* driving financial growth in your business.

## STAYING THE COURSE: HANDLING THE SPIRAL AND INTERRUPTING MIDDLE ZONE REGRESSION

One of the most important truths I've learned, both personally and through coaching clients, is that growth through self-leadership is not a straight line. You don't summit the mountain and stay there effortlessly. Real transformation comes with ebbs and flows. Some days you're flying. Other days something knocks you sideways—a failed contract, a conversation that doesn't go well, an old trigger that catches you off guard—and you find yourself slipping back toward old habits or fears.

In those moments, the key is not to dwell on what's happened. It's to focus on recovery. No matter how close you get to Impossible Freedom, Middle Zone thinking may still surface from time to time. But you can recognize it sooner, interrupt the pattern faster, and climb your way back with more self-awareness and grace.

That's where the idea of the "first rung" of a ladder comes in. Imagine you've slid into a trough. Maybe you're feeling stuck, overwhelmed, self-critical, or panicked about something in your business. In that trough, it can be hard to see the next step, let alone the summit. But you don't need to climb the whole ladder right away. You just need to reach for the first rung—a small, embodied action that reconnects you to your inner steadiness.

For me, it's a walk in nature. If I'm spiraling, overwhelmed, or doubting myself, stepping outside and moving my body always helps me regulate my nervous system. It gets me out of my head and into my body, where my inner knowing and truth lives. This one simple act, my first rung, has stopped my spiral more times than I can count. For others, it might be a breathing practice, journaling about your "why," sitting in meditation, gardening, or dancing in the kitchen. Whatever your first rung is, know it. Use it. Let it anchor you.

Some of the most common triggers for regression are what I call Middle Zone pitfalls, those sneaky patterns that pull you away from Ascended Possibility and back into fear-based thoughts and behaviors. Time Leaks are a big one. When you stop paying attention to where your time and energy are going and let your calendar overwhelm you, it's likely because you're triple-booked and slammed with obligations that weigh you down as a leader. Another pitfall is default decision-making: saying yes out of obligation, compromising because of fear, or shrinking your vision because the last bold move didn't land the way you hoped. Self-doubt, overthinking, and overidentifying with past failures can all trick you into believing you're back where you started.

Here's what I remind our clients when they experience those moments: Spiraling doesn't mean failure. It means you're evolving. Growth is an upward spiral, not a straight ascent. You may revisit familiar challenges, but you're meeting them with greater capacity, deeper insight, and stronger tools. You're not the same leader you were a year ago, or even a month ago. The terrain may look similar, but you're navigating it from a higher elevation. A mentor once said to me, "When it feels like the sky is falling, you're actually ascending."

A client of ours hit a setback when a major contract didn't come through. Almost immediately, she began questioning everything: her strategy, her team, even whether she had chosen the right ideal client. Fear took the wheel. But once we helped her ground back into her values and reconnect with her "why," clarity returned. The contract falling through wasn't a sign of failure; it was an invitation to refocus and recommit to the path she had already chosen.

What keeps you on an upward spiral isn't perfection—it's integration. That's why we don't teach a one-size-fits-all formula. Instead, we help leaders learn how to make Brave Decisions from their own Wild Wisdom, communicate with courage, and stay in relationships with themselves and others along the way. It's not about avoiding failure or eliminating mistakes. It's about leading yourself back again and again to what's true and having the inner resources and capacity to do that more quickly, with deeper trust each time.

So if you find yourself dipping, don't panic. Find the first rung on your ladder. Reach for it. Take that breath. Step into that walk. Put your hands on the earth. Hold a tree. Let your nervous system settle so your wisdom can rise. Then take your next step not from fear but from the steady knowing inside you that has never left.

## BRINGING YOUR VISION INTO FOCUS

Throughout our journey together, you've gained tools, insights, and practices that can help you reshape how you lead and live. You've seen what it takes to reclaim your time, build a more United Team, make Brave Decisions rooted in Wild Wisdom instead of old patterns, and have Courageous Conversations that move you forward. You've begun to recognize the pull of the Middle Zone and what it feels like to rise above it. Now it's time to bring those pieces together and claim what Impossible Freedom truly means to you.

This isn't about copying someone else's formula. It's about crafting your own. At Ascend Leadership Co., this is the work we help our clients do every day: translate clarity into action and align every part of their business and life with their energy and vision. Impossible Freedom isn't one-size-fits-all. It's personal to each individual, and it becomes real the moment you take full ownership of it. When founders and CEOs work with us, we help them name what matters most, assess where they are, and assemble a clear, integrated vision of the business and life they want to lead. We also give them the critical support and accountability they need to realize that vision.

To begin envisioning your own version of Impossible Freedom, grab a notebook or journal and answer the three sets of prompts below. Head outside into nature if you can and connect with your Wild Wisdom, the powerful inner knowing within you. Write from your heart, freely and unedited. Let your truth flow without judgment, as if no one will ever read it but you. Take your time. Allow honesty and curiosity to guide the way. You might even revisit these prompts a day or two later to see what new insights emerge.

## Part 1: Why Change? Why Now?

Let's start with truth and urgency for change. This isn't about working harder or doing more. It's about alignment, legacy, and *liberation.* Own your "why."

- Why is *now* the time for change?
- Why should you bother changing? Why is it urgent and nonnegotiable at this point in your journey? Why is this important to you?

- What are you no longer willing to tolerate in your business and life?
- A year from now, what would you regret if you don't do it or learn it now?
- What reasons do you have for *not* keeping things the same for another year or two?
- What makes this moment a wake-up call or a turning point?

## Part 2: Your Year of Impossible Freedom

Now imagine it's one year from today. Step into your future self's shoes and look back on the twelve months that just unfolded. In this vision, you've made courageous, aligned choices to climb out of the Middle Zone and ascend to Impossible Freedom. You're now leading and growing a business that fuels your life, not one that consumes it. You now feel fully lit up in business and life—*and* are driving more financial growth in your business. All of this felt impossible in the past, but now it's real.

Write a letter to your current self, who's embarking on this journey, from your future self, who's already lived in the next year. Use any or all of the prompts below to help you. Be audacious. Be detailed. Don't filter your vision. Write from your inner Wild Wisdom, like no one is watching. Let yourself be unapologetic and name and claim what you *really* want. This letter gets to be from you—to you.

Start your letter something like this:

Dear [insert your name], it is now [insert the date a year from now]. I can hardly wait to tell you about the amazing Year of Impossible Freedom we've had together. I'm so proud of you. Sit back and enjoy all there is for us to celebrate. Consider writing . . .

- What happened over the past year, personally and professionally, that made you feel happy and fulfilled with your progress.
- Your wins, results, and improvements.
- The challenges you solved and rose above.
- What made you feel lit up and alive, in your business and life.
- What you're most proud of.
- Who and what you're grateful for.
- Whatever else felt truly like success on your own terms.

Writing your letter and answering these prompts is the beginning of your path to Impossible Freedom. Pause here. Take a breath. You're closer than you might think to changing your life and creating what you truly want. And remember, there's no one-size-fits-all vision of Impossible Freedom. Your vision is the one that feels true to you and for you. Let it lead you forward.

## Part 3: The "Can'ts"—Call Out Your Perceived Limitations

As much as you want what you want, you likely also have fears and stories that still whisper "I can't" to you. For now, let's look at them head on. Then, in Chapter 8, we'll explore "can'ts" in more detail and how to defy them.

- What do you tell yourself (and maybe others) about why you *can't* change, grow, or pursue what you truly want?
- What voices or stories stand in the way of you following through? Why will this be too hard? Why can't you do this?
- What does your Wild Wisdom say about those fears and can'ts? How are they not true?

# YOUR REFLECT TO RISE JOURNAL

**Ascended Possibility:** This chapter introduces Ascended Possibility as a mindset that helps you take aligned action from vision rather than fear. Where in your business or life have you been solving problems from the same elevation that created them? What might shift if you start thinking from the elevated level of where you want to be?

**Middle Zone Thinking:** After reviewing the Middle Zone thinking vs. Ascended Possibility thinking tables in this chapter, which examples feel most familiar or revealing to you? Where do you notice yourself still operating from Middle Zone logic? What's one belief you're ready to reframe?

**Self-Leadership in Action:** Susie's story illustrates what happens when a leader stops mimicking inherited leadership styles and begins leading from her own truth. Where in your leadership are you still following someone else's model? What might it look like to step more fully into your own?

**The Ridgewalk Revisited:** This chapter describes how the Ridgewalk decision-making process shows up in moments of pressure, urgency, and uncertainty. When was the last time you applied this rhythm, whether consciously or not? What step felt strongest for you, and which needs more attention?

**Staying the Course:** The "first rung" concept offers a practical way to recover from Middle Zone spirals. What's one simple, embodied practice that helps you regulate and return to alignment when you're overwhelmed or stuck?

**Claiming Your Vision:** The chapter ends with an activity to help you envision what a year of Impossible Freedom would look like for you. If you've begun or completed the activity, what insights or surprises emerged for you? What support and accountability partners do you need to carry your vision forward in the weeks and months ahead?

**Taking Action:** What's one Brave Decision or Courageous Conversation that would reinforce your commitment to self-leadership right now? What support do you need to follow through?

**Community Connection:** Who in your network might benefit from the idea that leadership in business starts with self-leadership and that aligned, visionary thinking is a practice? What's one way you could share or model Ascended Possibility for others?

Get the free book companion with all reflection questions and exercises at ascendleadership.com/book.

# DEFYING CAN'T: FROM LIMITING BELIEFS TO LIMITLESS POTENTIAL

*By Nadine and Derek Nicholson*

---

**W**hen you're trapped in the Middle Zone, as so many high-performing leaders are, it silently shapes your thinking in ways that can be difficult to notice. Without realizing it, you start making decisions based not on what you want, but on what you believe you can't have. These limiting beliefs often go unchallenged, woven into your routines, reinforced by past experiences, and disguised as logic or responsibility. And they accumulate over time, weighing you down and influencing your choices, calendar, and sense of what's possible, often without you ever saying them out loud.

Much of our work with powerhouse leaders is helping them discover that they *can*. The turning point often comes when they move from Middle Zone thinking to Ascended Possibility, the space of alignment, clarity, and choice we explored in

Chapter 7. That shift is almost always marked by a single realization: *This belief I've been carrying about my limits isn't true.*

That's when everything starts to change.

In Chapter 2, we introduced Time Mastery as the first Leadership Pillar of the Impossible Freedom Equation. We explored six key elements that define it, including two that will be of particular importance in this chapter: eradicating your Say/Do Gap and defying "can't." We also shared the Say/Do Gap Eradicator, a powerful exercise to help you close the gap between what you *say* matters and what your calendar reflects. One of the steps in that exercise was to identify the beliefs that start with "I can't." Then, at the end of Chapter 7, you began clarifying your personal vision of Impossible Freedom, including answering three prompts about your "can'ts" and perceived limitations.

It's time to go deeper.

There's nothing more freeing than realizing you are not as stuck or limited as you thought you were. Defying "can't" is the heart and soul of your ascent to Impossible Freedom. In this chapter, we'll walk you through it, step-by-step. You'll choose one belief that's been holding you back and work through it using a simple, proven process that has helped leaders just like you move past old limits and open new levels of Ascended Possibility. By the time you finish, you'll have not only challenged that belief but also opened the door to leading and living from a place of truth instead of fear.

Here's how it works:

1. **Identify the "can't."** What belief is weighing you down or keeping you stuck?
2. **Question if it's true.** Where did this belief come from, and is it actually real?

3. **Explore possible solutions.** What alternative options might exist if you look at this differently?
4. **Shift to "How can I?"** What becomes possible when you move from resigned to curious?
5. **Give yourself permission to act.** What are you finally ready to allow yourself to do, be, have, see, and say?

Each step will be paired with real examples drawn from our clients—leaders who once believed they couldn't who now lead with clarity, confidence, and conviction. These transformations didn't come from working harder. They came from thinking differently. From breaking out of Middle Zone patterns and moving into the possibilities they had previously ruled out.

By the end of this chapter, you'll understand what it means to defy "can't" and feel the shift beginning to take root in yourself. It's like catching the first breath of clean air after being underwater or seeing the trail open up after miles of climbing in a dense forest. A belief that's been holding you back will loosen its grip, and in that open space, you'll catch sight of the freedom that's been within reach all along, ready for you to claim.

## STEP 1: IDENTIFY THE "CAN'T"— NAMING THE WEIGHT

There's a moment that happens with nearly every client we work with. Sometimes it shows up in the first conversation. Other times, it doesn't surface until we're well into our time together. But when it does, it's unmistakable.

We'll be exploring their vision: what they really want for both their business and their life. They'll begin to imagine a more ascended version of success that includes more space, joy, health, growth, and impact. And then, almost without realizing it, they'll shrink the vision back down:

- "I can't take Fridays off."
- "I can't trust my team to handle it the way I can."
- "I can't have both freedom *and* growth."
- "I can't stop managing my own calendar."
- "I can't step back right now; it's too risky."
- "I can't slow down. People are counting on me."

These "I can't" statements often sound responsible. Logical. Even admirable. But they're not the voice of truth. They're the voice of conditioning shaped by high-pressure environments, reinforced by a culture that rewards over-functioning and self-sacrifice, that's rarely questioned because it feels so familiar.

To the person saying it, "I can't" feels like a wall. Firm. Final. Immovable.

But it's not a wall. It's a weight. And that weight is heavy. It shows up in the tightness in your chest when your calendar is overbooked again. In the way you hesitate to delegate, even though your team is capable. In the internal tug-of-war between your goals and your well-being.

Here's what we've learned after working with, alongside, and in service of founders and CEOs for more than three decades: The weight you're feeling is not the weight of your business itself. The weight is *your belief about what's possible within your business*. These beliefs are shaped by past experiences, justified by results, and reinforced by the people around you. But still beliefs, not facts. And that's good news because beliefs can change.

One of our clients said it best after a breakthrough moment: "I don't need to carry the mountain to climb it." But before you can begin your climb, you need to name the load you're carrying.

That's why one of the most frequent activities we do with our clients is help them identify their Say/Do Gap and why we're returning to it in this chapter after exploring it as part of Time Mastery in Chapter 2.

When you say, "My health is a top priority," but you're skipping meals, canceling doctor appointments, having no time to pee, overcommitting, and pushing through exhaustion, that's a Say/Do Gap. When you say, "I want to be more present with my family," but your business consumes your evenings and weekends, that's a Say/Do Gap.

These gaps don't just reflect misalignment. They increase the weight of your "can'ts" because deep down, you know something's off. The dissonance grows. And with it, the belief that nothing can change.

The Say/Do Gap is also more than a mismatch. It's a signal revealing where Time Mastery is missing. Time Mastery isn't about productivity hacks or squeezing more into an already overloaded day. It's about aligning your decisions about your time with who and what you value most so your calendar becomes a reflection of your highest truth, not your perceived obligations. When you master your time, you're not only efficient; you're also intentional and grounded. You lead from clarity instead of reactivity.

And that's why this first step to defy your "can't" matters so much. When we help our clients name their "can'ts," we're not pointing out failure. We're shining a light on the exact place their leadership is ready to evolve because once the limiting belief is visible, its control over you can be dismantled.

Table 4 presents some of the most common time- and energy-related "can'ts" our clients have shared with us, along with the new realities they claimed once they challenged those beliefs. Not every statement begins with the words "I can't" or "I can," but each one reflects the transformation that happens when a leader defies their personal "can't."

Defying "can't" doesn't happen in isolation. Each transformation you see in Table 4 began when a client named their "can't" and then worked with us to shift it. In the table's "After" column, the results are described in the leader's own voice, speaking directly to us—personal, specific, and rooted in partnership. As you read through these examples, notice which ones resonate most with you and which could have come straight from your own thoughts or experience.

**Table 4.** From "I Can't" to "I Can"—Real Transformations in Time and Energy.

| Before ("I Can't") | After ("I Can") |
| --- | --- |
| I'm working too many hours and still not seeing the financial results I want. | In the last year, you helped me cut six hundred hours from my schedule and double my revenue. |
| My time gets hijacked, and I don't know how to protect it. | You helped me really challenge some of the stories that I told myself about what's important and where I should be spending my time. I now have control over my time again. |
| I can't remember the last time I took a real vacation, let alone enjoyed it. | You helped me take more vacation than ever and actually enjoy it. And my revenue went up, not down. |
| It feels like my business is draining the life out of me. | You helped me turn my business into something that fuels my life instead of drains it. |

*(Continued)*

**Table 4.** (*Continued*)

| Before ("I Can't") | After ("I Can") |
|---|---|
| When I'm working, I feel like I'm neglecting my kids. When I'm with my kids, I feel like I'm neglecting my business. | You helped me fill my own cup and take care of myself without guilt. I'm more present with my family, and my profits continue to increase. I'm a better human being, a better mother, and a better business owner. |
| I'm constantly running at full speed because if I don't, things will fall apart. | You helped me see that I'm the number one asset in my life and business. Without regular maintenance and support, it will be me who falls apart. |

## Your Turn: Choose One "Can't"

Pause here and take a moment to reflect. What's one belief you've been carrying, quietly or loudly, that starts with "I can't"? Don't overthink it. Choose one that feels especially true, or especially heavy. If you completed the Say/Do Gap Eradicator in Chapter 2 or the reflective questions in Chapter 7, return to your answers.

Write down one "can't" now.

You'll carry this belief through the rest of the chapter. This is the one you'll work through, step-by-step. You don't need to solve it yet. For now, you just need to name it and bring it with you into the next step.

## STEP 2: QUESTION THE TRUTH OF YOUR "CAN'T"—SURFACING THE STORIES

Once you've named a belief that's holding you back, it's tempting to stop there, to treat it as a fixed limitation and move on. But if you want to change how you lead your business and yourself, this is the moment to lean in. Naming your "can't" is only the starting point. The real work begins when you examine it.

When we ask clients to write down their "can'ts," they often state these beliefs with absolute certainty. There's no hesitation. Yet when we pause and ask, "Is that actually true?" the conversation transforms. Many realize they've never considered that question before.

A surprising number of "can'ts" aren't grounded in hard evidence. They're shaped by outdated thinking, past experiences, untested assumptions, and inherited expectations. These beliefs may have once served a purpose, but now they restrict what's possible.

In this step, you bring the stories you've told yourself (or absorbed from others) to the surface. This isn't about pretending everything is possible. Some "can'ts" are rooted in genuine constraints: a five-foot-tall person is unlikely to play in the NBA, someone recovering from knee surgery can't (yet) go on a strenuous hike, and a leader onboarding a new team may need to stay closely involved until the group is ready to fly. Honoring these realities is part of aligned self-leadership.

But most "can'ts" that keep leaders stuck aren't legitimate limits. They're internalized narratives that only hold power if you never stop to question them. By examining them, you weaken their grip. You start poking holes in the plot, noticing how you've miscast yourself, and making space for new ways of thinking and leading to emerge.

Table 5 offers examples of how unexamined "can't" beliefs show up in practice and what happens when leaders challenge them. Remember that the "after" column captures the words our clients used to describe the real transformations they experienced through our work together.

**Table 5.** From "I Can't" to "I Can"—Real Transformations in Decision-Making and Strategic Clarity.

| Before ("I Can't") | After ("I Can") |
| --- | --- |
| I make decisions from fear, pressure, or urgency, or I get paralyzed and don't make them at all. | You helped me make decisions from a place of inner power and self-trust, not fear. |
| I struggle to make tough personal decisions and often delay or overthink them. | You helped me make tough personal decisions with confidence, speed, and precision. My decision fatigue is gone. |
| I feel like I have to apologize for taking up space or being in charge. I'm not leading from a place of personal authority. | You helped me show up unapologetically and in more control of my business and life. |
| I dislike social media, but I'm stuck having to use it to grow my business. | You helped me use social media in a way that is more natural and authentic to me. |
| I have my go-to strategies for handling challenges, but they aren't working. I need to do something different, but I'm just not sure what. | You helped me navigate challenges with clarity and confidence while still honoring my relationships and values. |

## Your Turn: Question Your "Can't"

Take a closer look at the "can't" you identified in Step 1. Ask yourself:

- Is this still true today? How do you know, and what tells you that?
- Have I ever tested it or just accepted it as fact?
- Where did this belief come from?
- Is it something I genuinely believe or something I inherited from the culture, people, or systems around me?

Write out your answers without editing or overthinking. Be curious, not critical. You're not trying to solve the belief yet. You're simply trying to understand it.

Clarity comes before courage, and this is how you begin to loosen the grip of a belief that no longer serves you. Let's keep going.

## STEP 3: EXPLORE POSSIBLE SOLUTIONS— OPENING TO ALTERNATIVES

Once you begin to question a "can't," the foundation that held it up for so long begins to crumble. What once felt rigid loosens, and a little light gets in. This is the moment when something new becomes possible, not because your circumstances have changed, but because your perspective has. We call this the "I Can" moment. It's your first taste of what Impossible Freedom truly brings:

- An identity built on alignment rather than over-functioning.
- A life that honors both your goals and your well-being.
- A version of leadership that allows for space, presence, and ease.

For many of our clients, this is an unfamiliar feeling. They're used to solving problems by pushing harder. They're used to proving their worth through nonstop effort, so when we invite them to consider alternatives, to look for small but meaningful shifts, they sometimes hesitate. It feels too easy. Too soft. Too unfamiliar.

But here's the truth: The goal of this step isn't to overhaul your entire business or life. It's to open a door. To allow yourself to ask: "What else might be possible here? What's a gentler, smarter, more aligned way forward?"

When you begin to explore solutions, you're not committing to anything yet. You're simply allowing your imagination and leadership capacity to expand. You're stepping out of a reactive mindset and into creative ownership.

This is where you move from fatigue to fuel.

When leaders stop trying to earn their freedom and start designing for it, success becomes sustainable. They give themselves permission to rest without guilt. They reconnect to the work they love. They stop waiting for things to get better and start creating rhythms and systems that support their energy. And in doing so, they reclaim more than time—they reclaim themselves.

Table 6 presents some of the personal breakthroughs our clients have experienced when they stopped leading from depletion and started leading from a place of strong boundaries.

**Table 6.** From "I Can't" to "I Can"—Real Transformations in Well-Being and Boundaries.

| Before ("I Can't") | After ("I Can") |
| --- | --- |
| It's normal for my business to overtake my life and to be up worrying in the middle of the night. | You helped me create a healthier, happier path so I can show up at my best in the different areas of my life. I'm leaps and bounds ahead of where I was before. |
| I believe to grow my business I have to put my own well-being last. More hustle means more success. | You helped me see that business growth doesn't have to come at the cost of my own well-being. Now I work smarter, trust my instincts, and my business is thriving without burning me out in the process. |

*(Continued)*

**Table 6.** (*Continued*)

| Before ("I Can't") | After ("I Can") |
|---|---|
| When I'm not working, I feel guilt that I should be working. I can't relax and be present with myself or the people around me. | You helped me no longer carry guilt when I'm not working. I have the space and confidence to prioritize me without having to be everything to everyone. I feel more present wherever I am. |
| I can't step back without losing momentum or missing big opportunities. | You helped me step back, trust my team more, work less, and land our biggest contract ever. |
| I know this pace isn't sustainable, especially for my health, but I don't know what to change. I feel like my life is slipping away. | You helped me take myself off the back burner and stop sacrificing my health. I now have the emotional, mental, and physical bandwidth to actually enjoy my life. |

## Your Turn: Open to New Possibilities

Before you can shift your mindset to new possibilities, you need to know that the "I can" stage depends on your ability to adopt a new belief rooted in "I can." Now return to the belief you're working through. You've named it. You've questioned it. Now it's time to explore what could come next.

Ask yourself:

- What would it be like to soften my belief?
- Am I open to the idea that my "I can't" beliefs are not real or true?
- Am I willing to believe the possibility that I can?

Now ask yourself:

- What's one small change I can make that would move me toward the possibility that I'm creating by defying can't?

- What would become available to me if I chose to restore myself on a regular basis rather than just react to my circumstances?

This is not about pretending you have total control over every variable in your business or life. It's about reclaiming the influence you *do* have and using it to lead from a place that's honest, intentional, and sustainable.

Write down one idea. One alternative. One possible solution. It doesn't have to be perfect. It just has to be yours.

Let's keep going. You're getting closer.

## STEP 4: SHIFT TO "HOW CAN I?"— CLEARING THE TRAIL

Once you've named your limiting belief, questioned its truth, and explored new possibilities, it's time to ask a different kind of question that turns awareness into action: "How can I?"

This question moves your energy from feeling boxed in to looking for tangible ways forward. It invites creativity, resourcefulness, and bolder thinking. Most importantly, it reminds you that leadership isn't about carrying the full load yourself. It's about setting up the conditions that allow new outcomes to take shape.

We see this step take many forms. Sometimes it sparks a personal priority: "How can I reclaim my mornings? How can I take a real vacation this year?" Other times, it leads to structural or strategic decisions: "How can I design my business to support the life I actually want to live?"

One powerful lens for this step is your team. In Chapter 3, we introduced the second Leadership Pillar of the Impossible Freedom Equation, United Team, along with the concept of the Support Gap—the disconnect between having a team and being supported by it. Mastering your time won't get you to Impossible Freedom if your team isn't equipped to support you at the right level. For many founders and CEOs, the Support Gap quietly stalls growth no matter how hard or smart they work. They may hire people, delegate tasks, and put systems in place, yet still find themselves carrying too much. Decisions bottleneck at the top. Problems land back on their desk. The team exists, but true support is missing.

When leaders bring "How can I?" to this context, their questions often sound like:

- "How can I build a team I can truly trust?"
- "How can I step out of the weeds without everything falling apart?"
- "How can I restructure roles so the business no longer depends on me?"
- "How can I simplify processes and stop doing things that don't add value?"

These are more than hypothetical musings. They're gateways to concrete solutions that get you out of the Middle Zone.

Of course, not every "How can I?" involves team restructuring. For you, this step might mean reworking your schedule, initiating a Brave Decision or Courageous Conversation, automating a draining task, or setting a new boundary. Whatever form it takes, the key is reclaiming agency and taking intentional steps toward the future you want.

Table 7 captures examples of the tangible leadership breakthroughs that emerge when leaders stop only asking "Can I?" and start asking "How can I?"

**Table 7.** From "I Can't" to "I Can"—Real Transformation in Leadership and Team Dynamics.

| Before ("I Can't") | After ("I Can") |
|---|---|
| I don't have anyone to help me talk about difficult team dynamics or high-stakes leadership challenges. | You helped me have a safe place to talk through stressful team situations and the clarity to know what to do next. |
| Difficult conversations leave me anxious, and I avoid them even when I shouldn't. | You helped me navigate tough conversations with confidence, kindness, and firmness. |
| I keep hiring reactively or settling for "good enough" when it comes to my team. | You helped me make strategic hires that strengthened and united my team. |
| There are critical gaps in my leadership team, but I'm not sure how to fix them. | You helped me close every gap in my leadership structure. |
| The business can't function without me constantly managing it. | You helped me trust my leadership team completely, and they've stepped up in ways I never imagined. |

## Your Turn: Ask "How Can I?"

Now it's your turn to move from possibility to practice. Take the belief you've been working with and the ideas you began exploring in Step 3. Ask yourself:

- How can I begin to act on this?
- What kind of support would I need to make this change?
- What systems or structures need to shift so I'm not doing it all myself?

Write down one "How can I?" question that feels actionable and true. Let it guide your next decision and begin walking the trail you've just cleared.

You're almost there. Let's take the final step.

## STEP 5: GIVE YOURSELF PERMISSION— CLAIMING YOUR FREEDOM

By the time our clients reach this stage, something has already changed. They've named a belief that was keeping them stuck. They've questioned it, explored new possibilities, and started asking practical questions. And still, one final barrier remains, the most stubborn one of all.

Permission.

For many high-achieving leaders, the issue isn't capacity or strategy. It's self-authorization. They don't wait for permission from their board, their team, or their family. They wait for permission from themselves.

They say, "I'll slow down after this next project. I'll rest once I've hit the next revenue goal. I'll step back once everything's running smoothly."

But that moment never comes. Because the to-do list never ends. The growth never stops. And the conditions are never perfect. This is why the final step of the Defy Can't process is so important. It's the shift from planning to choosing. From intention to ownership. From waiting to allowing.

You don't need to earn your freedom. You need to claim it.

We've seen what happens when leaders give themselves this permission. They stop proving and start living. They step into a new rhythm that honors their values and protects their energy. They lead with more conviction, more joy, and more space. And their business begins to thrive in ways it never did before.

This isn't just about better leadership. It's about designing a life and legacy that reflects who you really are. Table 8 shows what that can look like.

**Table 8.** From "I Can't" to "I Can" Real Transformation in Purpose and Passion.

| Before ("I Can't") | After ("I Can") |
| --- | --- |
| I'm overworked, worn out, and feeling I should just throw in the towel and retire. | You helped me love what I do again. I got my passion back for my business while also finding more time for me too. |
| I'm so used to pushing that I've lost touch with what I really want. | You helped me get honest with myself about what I truly want and follow through instead of treating it as out of reach. |
| I've lost hope that there's a better way to do this. | You helped me have hope again. I know there's a different way of doing things, and I'm making it happen. |
| I'm afraid to dream bigger because I don't believe it's possible. | You helped me have the courage to dream bigger, and my dreams are becoming my reality. |
| I want to build something that lasts, but I don't know how to make space for that vision. | You helped me take back my time to build a legacy and live the life I've always wanted. |

## Your Turn: Give Yourself Permission

Take one more look at the belief you've been working through. You've done the work to see it clearly. You've loosened its hold. You've opened to new options. Now it's time to ask:

- What am I ready to allow?
- What have I been waiting for to give myself permission?
- What would change if I stopped postponing and started living from alignment now?

Write down one statement that begins with "I give myself permission to . . ." Make it personal. Make it honest. Let it reflect what you're truly ready to claim.

You don't need to be more productive, more accomplished, or more prepared. You're ready now. This is the final step. And it's also the first step toward a new way of leading and living.

## A RALLYING CRY FOR EVERY LEADER WHO WANTS MORE

You began this chapter with a belief that felt immovable, a quiet "can't" that's been shaping your choices and defining your limits. You're leaving it with something far more empowering: the knowledge that those types of limits are never the whole truth.

This is what it means to move from limiting beliefs to limitless potential. Not in theory but in lived reality. One choice at a time. One act of permission at a time. One closed Say/Do Gap at a time.

Defying "can't" is your rallying cry. It's not a one-time breakthrough but an ongoing leadership practice. It's a way to stay honest with yourself when you feel stuck, overloaded, or out of alignment. It invites you to pause and ask: *Is this a true limit, or am I holding myself back by not choosing differently?*

When a new "can't" emerges, you can return to this simple, repeatable prompt:

1. My "can't" is . . .
2. Why I believe I can't:
3. Is it true? What else might be possible?
4. How can I . . .?
5. I give myself permission to . . .

You don't have to work through these steps in isolation. Every transformation in this chapter came from leaders we coached who had a trusted partner in us to walk alongside them. For you, it might be a peer, family member, or mentor who can hold up a mirror to your potential and the conditions that affect it. Sometimes one honest conversation with someone who truly sees you is all it takes to open a door you didn't know was there.

And here's the deeper truth: Every time you defy a "can't," you expand what's possible. You reclaim your energy, your vision, your voice. You lead from clarity instead of fear. And you prove—first to yourself and then to everyone around you—that freedom isn't something to wait for. It's something you live, here and now.

So take your next step boldly. Carry the process with you like a compass: Name it. Question it. Open it. Ask it. Claim it. Repeat. Each time you do, you choose the path that prioritizes your well-being as fiercely as your business goals.

You don't have to carry the mountain to climb it. Start today. Defy one "can't." And step into the Impossible Freedom you've worked so hard to make possible.

# YOUR REFLECT TO RISE JOURNAL

**Leadership Practice:** This chapter positions defying "can't" as both a leadership practice and a way of living. How does this framing expand or change your understanding of what leadership requires?

**Workplace Culture:** The Middle Zone is described as a place where "can'ts" silently shape thinking and decisions over time. In what ways can workplace cultures unintentionally reinforce these "can'ts"? How can that culture be shifted?

**Framework Connection:** Defying "can't" is presented as part of the Say/Do Gap framework. How does focusing on a single "can't" address larger misalignments between what a leader values and how they spend their time?

**Inspiration:** This chapter draws on real examples from leaders across industries and contexts. Which example most impacts your own sense of what's possible and why?

**Personal Focus:** The authors describe defying "can't" as a tool you can use at any stage of your growth. Where do you think it has the greatest potential to impact you (e.g., in navigating change, pursuing growth, simplifying, reclaiming personal time)?

**Taking Action:** The transformations presented in this chapter were made possible through partnership rather than solo effort. Who's providing you with an external perspective right now (someone who can help you see possibilities you might be missing)? If you don't have that kind of partner, where could you find one?

**Community Connection:** Who in your network might benefit from learning the Defy Can't process? How could you share it with them in a way that feels natural and encouraging?

## CHAPTER 9

# NOT SOMEDAY, NOW: LIVING IN FREEDOM AND LEGACY

*By Nadine and Derek Nicholson*

You've traveled far since the first pages of this book. You began by naming and confronting the hidden costs of the Middle Zone: those draining Say/Do and Support Gaps, Time and Team Leaks, and the three Middle Zone leadership types that quietly stall progress. From there, you put the Impossible Freedom Equation to work, grounding your leadership in two powerful pillars: Time Mastery and United Team.

You didn't stop there. You activated the three Leadership Amplifiers of Wild Wisdom, Brave Decisions, and Courageous Conversations, each designed to deepen your clarity, empower your actions, and strengthen your relationships. You explored Ascended Possibility and Self-Leadership, learning how to lead from self-trust instead of self-doubt, and you began to defy "can't" by dismantling the self-imposed limits that once defined your edges.

Along the way, you practiced new patterns. You reclaimed energy you didn't realize you'd lost. You made bolder choices with more ease and less second-guessing. You saw that small shifts in how you lead your time, your team, and yourself can spark outsized impact not only in your business, but in your life.

But here's the truth: You can't climb higher (whether that's growing your business, creating space for yourself outside work, or nurturing a legacy you dream of) by relying on the same strategies that got you here. New levels of success require new tools for transformation and leadership. What served you in the past will not carry you to the peaks you now see from here.

And time, your most precious resource, isn't renewable. You can either seize every day with intention or let them slip through your fingers, one after another, until you wonder where they all went. Too many leaders keep pushing off the joy, adventure, and true freedom they thought their business would bring them, but someday isn't coming on its own. It comes now, if you choose it.

For us, this truth has been made real by life's wake-up calls, those moments that shake you out of autopilot and remind you how quickly things change. The loss of our parents, watching our son grow from a boy into a man seemingly overnight, even noticing the way our bodies respond differently to physical activity now than they did twenty years ago—these are all vivid reminders that time waits for no one.

Maybe you haven't had that kind of wake-up call yet, but you can feel the strain nevertheless. Your current level of busyness isn't sustainable, and deep down you know something has to give. You keep pushing harder, telling yourself that if you can just get through the next project or quarter, then you'll finally step back, take a break, and take care of yourself. But that moment never comes because something else always takes its place. For some leaders, the urgency to live and lead differently only comes after a personal wake-up call. For others, it can be built deliberately with the help of someone who holds up a mirror and shows what's at stake if they keep waiting.

Either way the choice you need to make is the same: Act now, not someday.

If you picture your journey as a climb, right now you're standing on a high ridge. The air is clearer here. You can see farther than you ever could in the Middle Zone, past the familiar valleys of overwork and overwhelm and into the expansive peaks of possibility. But this isn't the end of the climb. From this vantage point, you can spot the next summits that are calling to you. The question is no longer whether you can reach them. The question is whether you'll allow yourself to reach them.

That's the crossroads every leader faces when they realize staying in the Middle Zone is no longer an option, and it's the same one we named in the introduction: Are you ready to ascend?

## HOW TO SUSTAIN IMPOSSIBLE FREEDOM AS A PRACTICE

Impossible Freedom isn't a one-time achievement. It's a way of leading your time, team, and business that you strengthen every day through practice. Throughout this book, we've shown how our approach to leadership opens new possibilities and how the Impossible Freedom Equation provides the structure to turn those possibilities into reality:

- **Time Mastery:** Align your actions with your true priorities so your calendar reflects what matters most, not just what's most urgent.
- **United Team:** Build a cohesive support system that helps drive your vision forward and frees up your time, instead of relying too heavily on you to carry the load.
- **Wild Wisdom:** Tap into and trust your inner knowing, especially when external noise tries to cloud your judgment.
- **Brave Decisions:** Make bold and confident choices from your inner knowing, without fear or decision fatigue, even when the outcome isn't guaranteed.
- **Courageous Conversations:** Speak your needs, boundaries, and ideas with kindness and firmness, building stronger, more authentic relationships.

These pillars and amplifiers will lead you to Impossible Freedom, but only if you keep actively using them. The Middle Zone is always looking for a way back in, slipping in quietly as "just for now" compromises, overfilled calendars, and commitments to yourself that you keep pushing aside. Old habits resurface, bringing time scarcity, over-functioning, and avoidance patterns. The signs often hide in plain sight: You're stuck in chronic stress mode, unable to fully "turn off," never completely present, and constantly pulled in multiple directions. Guilt and resentment grow as you repeatedly sacrifice in the name of urgency, draining your health, relationships, and well-being.

One of the biggest Middle Zone culprits is the Time Myth, the paradox of believing you have all the time in the world while also feeling you never have enough time right now.

This dual belief fuels a cycle of delay as you tell yourself you'll act "once things settle down" or "after the next big project is done." These delays feel temporary and harmless, but they quietly open the door for the Middle Zone to trap you again. Each postponed conversation, deferred decision, or sidelined priority becomes another brick in the wall between where you are and where you want to be.

To stay out of the Middle Zone for good, you must invest in yourself and approach your self-leadership with intention:

- **Schedule regular Wild Wisdom check-ins**, guiding yourself to Brave Decisions that are aligned with your deepest values and vision.
- **Identify and close Say/Do Gaps** before they grow into patterns that drain your energy.
- **Proactively address Support Gaps** by evolving your team's roles, skills, and structures so they match the business you're leading today.
- **Initiate Courageous Conversations early** instead of waiting until a situation becomes urgent.
- **Revisit your vision of Impossible Freedom quarterly** so it stays fresh and relevant to where you are now, not where you were months ago.

The heart of sustaining Impossible Freedom is consistency. Value-driven decisions and actions awaken long-term resilience, shaping how you spend your time now and the legacy you're building for the future. When you treat your freedom as something you deserve, not something you have to earn, you make it unshakeable.

Sustaining Impossible Freedom also means recognizing that the journey never truly ends. Each summit you reach reveals new horizons, calling you to expand again. Sometimes that call is a reminder to return to a beginner's mindset, to approach Wild Wisdom not as something mastered but as something to encounter anew. For Nadine, this invitation came through Mother Nature when she committed to a six-month certification as a forest therapy guide. Her goal wasn't to collect another credential but to deepen her ability to listen, learn, and lead from her Wild Wisdom in elevated ways and guide others to do the same. This step represents what sustaining Impossible Freedom looks like in practice: continuing to grow, reengage, and stay open to new perspectives, even after years or decades of experience.

Impossible Freedom doesn't come at a finish line. It comes to you as a lived practice of ascent, where each peak prepares you for the next and every horizon opens space for more clarity, courage, and freedom.

## THE GIFT OF LEGACY THINKING AND PURPOSEFUL URGENCY

Once you've begun to pursue Impossible Freedom and commit to sustaining it, a new horizon comes into view that extends beyond the metrics and milestones of today. That horizon is your legacy.

Legacy isn't just about the tangible results you leave behind, like wealth or business assets. It's the imprint on the world you make through the way you invest your most precious resources: your time, energy, and presence. It's the ripple effect of your leadership on the people you lead, the communities you serve, and the industries you influence. It's the joy you create for yourself and others, and the example you set for how to live a life that's both ambitious and aligned.

For Nadine, the urgency to think about legacy came into sharp focus after her father's sudden passing just twenty-one days after his cancer diagnosis. The experience left her with what we call "purposeful urgency": a deep, steady resolve to say yes more often to her truest desires without waiting for a better time. It's not about frantic, panic-driven action. It's about choosing deliberately, knowing that the most important opportunities happen now, not someday.

Too often you miss this shift because you're still operating from a belief that personal sacrifice is the price of business success. You give up time with loved ones, your own health, and the moments that could bring you joy and happiness, assuming it's the only way to keep the business growing. In reality that trade-off undermines both the quality of your days in the present and the legacy you want to leave after you're gone.

Even when you recognize the cost, you might not see a way out without risking the success you've fought so hard for and the momentum you've built. Decision fatigue can weigh you down, sometimes leaving you paralyzed, unsure of which change to make first. You may feel isolated, as though it's all on you, particularly when you don't have a trusted, objective partner, mentor, or coach to help you see the bigger picture and make the tough calls with confidence and precision.

When you reach this point in your leadership, the success you've achieved already is no longer enough. You start asking different questions:

- What would make my life impossible to regret?
- What will remain when I'm no longer here?
- How do I want people to remember me?

The shift to legacy thinking and purposeful urgency changes something fundamental in your approach to business and living. Your priorities sharpen. The noise falls away. Your decisions become about short-term wins and long-term impact. You begin to measure success not only in profit or progress, but in the significance of the moments and contributions that will outlast you.

This is the true summit of leadership, where your climb leads you to a new vantage point while also forging a path others can follow. And like every other stage of this journey, you won't drift into it by accident. It's a choice you must make. A conscious decision to lead both for what you can achieve now and for what will continue to matter years from today. What a gift this is.

## KELLY TAYLOR'S LEGACY IN ACTION: FIVE LESSONS FOR LIVING AND LEADING WITH FREEDOM

Some lessons come from books. Others from experience. The most profound come from people. For us, one of those people was Kelly Taylor, our financial advisor, mentor, and dear friend. In February 2025, while we were writing this book, Kelly passed away unexpectedly at just forty-six years old. His loss was a devastating reminder that life is fragile and that the best time to make the changes you've been putting off is always now.

Kelly's influence reaches even further than the financial and strategic guidance he offered us. In fact, this book itself exists in part because of him. Kelly urged us to capture our leadership philosophy and frameworks into a form that could live beyond conversations, workshops, and client engagements. He believed our intellectual property—the ideas, practices, and lessons we had tested and refined—needed to be shared widely, not kept quietly within our coaching sessions. His encouragement planted the seed that eventually grew into these pages. In many ways, Kelly is not only present in the stories we tell here, but woven into the very reason this book came to life.

As a certified financial planner, Kelly managed wealth as a vehicle for helping people design lives where success is measured in more than numbers, but also in time, impact, and fulfillment. His version of Impossible Freedom was what he called "life design," and his favorite term for it was "work optional." He was a key influence on our journey to Impossible Freedom, shaping how we approached the Leadership Pillars and Leadership Amplifiers. He joined our United Team in 2009 at exactly the right moment, offering expertise we didn't have and anchoring our biggest decisions in both strategy and possibility. He was the kind of advisor who could talk mortgage refinancing one minute, then in the next remind you to write a letter to your family in case something ever happened to you.

Kelly's approach was as practical as it was visionary. Early in our work together, he guided us through estate planning and the creation of our first will, two critical steps we had delayed for years. He encouraged us to write "last letters" to our loved ones and, rather than storing them away for a distant future, to read them aloud while we're still here to see and feel their impact. Just weeks before his sudden and unexpected death, Kelly worked with us to design our work-optional plan that mapped out our financial goals and milestones from now until our nineties. It includes when we plan to scale back our business, when we plan to enter active retirement, and how we will ensure the years in between are filled with joy, family, rest, travel, and meaningful work.

As we have grieved Kelly's passing, we also found ourselves reflecting on the lessons he gave us over more than two decades of partnership and friendship. The following five lessons continue to influence our lives and how we hope you'll approach your own journey toward Impossible Freedom. Just as we've done in previous chapters by providing Reflect to Rise Journal questions, we invite you to pause with the questions included with each lesson. You can use them as personal journaling prompts or bring them into a group discussion. They are designed to help you move beyond inspiration into action, applying Kelly's wisdom directly to your own leadership and life.

1. **Brave Decisions shape your life's story.** Nearly twenty years ago, Nadine made the leap from a corporate executive role in strategic communications into her own executive leadership coaching business, a move that felt almost impossible at the time. Kelly helped make it possible, restructuring our finances to give her an eighteen-month runway to build sustainably. He reminded us that freedom requires courage but also strategy. The right planning turns a big risk into a big opportunity.

   *Reflective Question:* What's a decision you've been avoiding because it feels too risky? With the right support and plan, can it become your next defining moment?

2. **You are your number one asset.** Kelly often said, "The smartest investment you can make is in your own leadership development." He knew that without a strong leader at the helm, no business or life can thrive. His encouragement was unwavering.

   *Reflective Question:* What's one way you can prioritize your growth as much as you prioritize the growth of your business? Remember, you're the engine that drives both.

3. **Build wealth for options, not just security.** When Derek lost both his parents within seven months of each other, Kelly helped him take a two-year sabbatical from working so he had time to grieve and manage their estate. This also allowed Derek to be a stay-at-home dad and spend precious time with our son and volunteer at his school, which was a dream of Derek's. Kelly showed us that wealth is about more than security; it's about creating options to live your "someday" dreams now.

   *Reflective Question:* What's something you've always wanted to do but keep putting off? What resources do you have to make space for it now?

4. **Take calculated risks that align with your vision.** When Derek was on sabbatical, we decided to buy a vacation rental near Banff, Alberta. This was a "someday" dream and big leap for us, but Kelly's guidance and financial modeling gave us the clarity and confidence to move forward. That property now pays for itself, generates income, and has doubled in value.

   *Reflective Question:* What calculated risk, if taken with intention and alignment to your long-term goals, could catalyze your growth in a new and exciting direction?

5. **Protect the freedom you're building.** Kelly believed growth and protection went hand in hand. He guided us

to think about all the possible risk scenarios (like getting cancer or being disabled without an ability to work) and helped us create a robust risk management plan for those scenarios, ensuring our work-optional life would be as secure as possible for decades.

**Reflective Question:** How are you protecting the freedom you're building (including your time, health, relationships, and financial stability) so you don't have to rebuild from scratch after a setback?

Kelly's legacy is an unmistakeable call to action. Don't wait to shape the life you want. Time is your most valuable currency; spend it with intention. Take the leap. Say the words to make it real. Protect your freedom fiercely. And judge your success not only by the numbers you track, but also by the moments, impact, and well-being you create along the way. That's how you embrace what truly matters.

## WHAT WILL MATTER

When we gathered to celebrate Kelly's life, one moment really stayed with us. A family member of Kelly's read Michael Josephson's poem "What Will Matter." It cuts straight to the heart of what we've been discussing in this book: that the truest measure of a person isn't found in what you accumulate, but in the difference you make. Here's the poem in full:

**What Will Matter**
*By Michael Josephson*
Ready or not, someday it will all come to an end.
There will be no more sunrises, no minutes, hours,
    or days.

Your wealth, fame, and power will shrivel to irrelevance.

Your grudges, resentments, frustrations, and jealousies will finally disappear.

So too, your hopes, ambitions, plans, and to-do lists will expire.

The wins and losses that once seemed so important will fade away.

It will not matter where you came from or what side of the tracks you lived on at the end.

It will not matter whether you were beautiful or brilliant.

Even your gender and skin color will be irrelevant.

So what will matter? How will the value of your days be measured?

What will matter is not what you bought, but what you built, not what you got, but what you gave.

What will matter is not your success, but your significance.

What will matter is not what you learned, but what you taught.

What will matter is every act of integrity, compassion, courage, or sacrifice that enriched, empowered, or encouraged others to emulate your example.

What will matter is not your competence, but your character.

What will matter is not how many people you knew, but how many will feel a lasting loss when you're gone.

What will matter is not your memories, but the memories of those who loved you.

What will matter is how long you will be remembered, by whom, and for what.

Living a life that matters doesn't happen by accident.

It's not a matter of circumstance, but of choice.
Choose to live a life that matters.[4]

Josephson's poem leaves us with a piercing question: *In the end, what will matter?* It encourages you to examine how you're living and leading in the present, and what this makes you feel about yourself and the time you're spending on this earth. It also echoes the core themes we've explored throughout this book:

- **Building over buying:** Legacy comes from what you contribute, not what you acquire.
- **What lasts over what's loud:** Balance sheets and awards are fleeting on their own; what endures is the purpose behind them and the meaning they spark for you and others.
- **Choice over circumstance:** A life that matters is designed intentionally, not left to chance.

This is the soul of Impossible Freedom. It's about making deliberate choices today that align with your values and fuel your joy. It's being formed right now in the way you spend your limited time, lead your team, and show up for the people and pursuits that are important to you. Your legacy isn't a far-off milestone you'll get to "once everything is in place," and it won't be achieved in a single grand moment of accomplishment. It will be written in your daily actions.

---

[4] Michael Josephson, "What Will Matter," *Michael Josephson's What Will Matter: Quotes, Insights, & Images About a Life That Matters* blog, 2003, accessed January 22, 2026, https://whatwillmatter.com/2011/10/what-will-matter-745-3/. Used with permission from Michael Josephson, author and founder of CHARACTER COUNTS!

Importantly, Impossible Freedom doesn't mean life suddenly becomes easy or perfect. Alongside the joy and clarity, there will always be moments of shadow and uncertainty. Facing mortality, wrestling with fear and failure, and sitting with the grief of losing loved ones are all part of the human experience, no matter how free or fulfilled you may feel.

What changes with Impossible Freedom is not the absence of darkness, but the way you move through it. With Wild Wisdom as your compass and Ascended Possibility as your horizon, you find the courage to breathe into the mystery of the unknown instead of avoiding it. You learn to hold both gratitude and fear at once, to see the preciousness of life more clearly because of its limits, not in spite of them. In this way, Impossible Freedom is less about achieving a perfect state than it is about experiencing a grounded way of living. It equips you to navigate the shadows with presence, resilience, and optimism, even when the path ahead isn't fully lit.

## A SACRED READING AND OPENING TO NADINE'S WILD WISDOM IN GRIEF

Up to this point in the chapter, Derek and I have been telling the story about Kelly together, but this next piece comes from me because it reflects my own journey through grief and how Wild Wisdom guided me in the most unexpected ways.

In the months after Kelly's passing, I felt called to create a sacred ceremony for myself to sit with the grief, the mystery, and the lessons his life and legacy have left behind for me. I took an early draft of this chapter into the forest near our home to a bench I have visited countless times over the years. That morning the air was thick with fog, softening and blurring the edges of everything around me. On the backrest of the bench I sat on was an inscription I had seen before but never noticed so deeply: "In every walk with nature one receives far more than she seeks." —John Muir

Sitting there, I welcomed my Wild Wisdom, allowing myself to listen for what it wanted to tell me. I read this chapter aloud, my voice breaking at points, my throat tightening, and my tears flowing. With every pause, I leaned into the silence of the forest, asking what was waiting to be revealed. The forest held me safe and urged me to breathe in the fog, to take in the mystery of not knowing what comes next.

By the time I reached the final lines, I heard an unmistakable message rise within me: *Thank you for touching my life, for helping me see through the fog, and for having the courage to share my wisdom with the world. I am grateful.* It felt like my own spirit rising to speak with Kelly's spirit, carried through the presence of Mother Nature herself.

In that moment, John Muir's words came alive: I had gone seeking closure and received far more—a sense of connection, healing, and gratitude much like the "last letters" Kelly had encouraged us to write to our loved ones. This was my last letter to Kelly, written after his passing, yet not too late for him to receive it with the support of Mother Nature. A circle closed between us, his voice merging with my own in grief and creativity.

This sacred ceremony became a reminder that legacy is not abstract or distant. It lives in the words we share, in the mentoring we receive, in the healing we allow ourselves, in the rituals we create, and in the courage to bring our wisdom forward even through loss, tears, and the unknown. Kelly helped me see that freedom is not something we simply achieve; it's something we experience. With all its beauty. With all its grief. This book is just one tributary of Kelly's much larger impact, and it exists because he believed in me and refused to let me postpone becoming the person who could write it.

***This one's for you, Kelly. For seeing the bridge from someday to now and walking me across it.***

# YOUR FINAL INVITATION

At the heart of this book, and our work with leaders, is a simple truth: You don't have to choose between success and self. You get to have both. You get to grow your business and live your life in a way that is deeply fulfilling, unapologetically yours, and free of the constant trade-offs you once believed were unavoidable.

What we really do is help leaders redefine success. We help them stop chasing the version handed to them by culture, industry, or comparison, and start defining success on their own terms. A client's journey typically starts in self-doubt, making decisions from fear, scarcity, or the pressure to keep up with someone else's expectations. But over time we help business leaders come to make choices from self-trust, guided by clarity, grounded in their values, and unshaken by external noise. That is the ascent to Impossible Freedom.

One of the most persistent barriers we see is the guilt leaders feel about investing in their own leadership development. Many successful entrepreneurs spend freely on new equipment, facilities, vehicles, and their employees' professional development but hesitate when it comes to their own growth, as if it's indulgent or undeserved. The truth can't be overstated: YOU are the number one asset in your business and life. Without your vision, energy, and well-being, nothing else can operate at its best. Investing in yourself is not a luxury; it's a prerequisite for sustained success for you and everyone whose lives you impact. We cannot emphasize this enough.

For many leaders, even taking time off feels impossible without guilt, or without bracing for an avalanche of work and problems that will be waiting when you return. That looming price keeps you tethered to the grind, reinforcing the belief that stepping away will only make things harder, which is why, for many, it takes a moment of reckoning to finally break the pattern.

While many leaders are moved to action by a personal wake-up call (a health scare, the loss of a loved one, or an experience where the cost of "business as usual" becomes too high), you don't have to wait for crisis to change course—and you shouldn't! No matter your motivation, a skilled coach or mentor can help you see what's at stake and create the momentum you need to act now, nurturing a sense of purposeful urgency that keeps you moving forward before opportunity slips away.

As we've shown in these pages, Impossible Freedom isn't a someday dream. It's a leadership decision. You've seen why so many powerhouse founders and CEOs get trapped in the Middle Zone, even after hitting revenue goals, building large teams, and checking every box of traditional success. You've now learned how to break free from what's holding you back by applying the Impossible Freedom Equation to reclaim your time, energy, and joy while reaching new heights in your business.

Here's our final call to you, from both of us, as partners in this work and in life: Stop waiting. Stop postponing the life you've worked so hard to make possible. Ten years from now, your biggest regret will not be a missed business goal or an achievement you didn't chase. Ten years from now your biggest regret would be not choosing your health, energy, aliveness, and relationships now.

Choose today to . . .

- **Live fully**, in a way that reflects your truth, values, and real priorities.
- **Grow your business** intentionally and sustainably so it supports rather than consumes you.

- **Leave a legacy** that matters, built in daily actions, not distant finish lines.

Your time on this earth is finite, and you're standing at a crossroads. The path to Impossible Freedom is wide open before you. The air is clearer here, the view more expansive, and the next summit calls. The question is no longer whether you can reach it. The question is whether you will choose to.

It's time to ascend. Not someday, now.

# A GLOSSARY OF ASCEND LEADERSHIP CO.'S KEY TERMS

**Brave Decisions™**

One of three Leadership Amplifiers. Bold, confident choices rooted in inner wisdom—not external pressure, performance, or "shoulds." Brave Decisions turn clarity into commitment, moving you from insight to action even when the stakes are high or the outcome uncertain. Practicing Brave Decisions consistently builds momentum, strengthens self-trust, and reinforces the confidence to lead with conviction.

**Courageous Conversations™**

One of three Leadership Amplifiers. Courageous Conversations mean saying the hard things with kindness and firmness, creating connection, accountability, and integrity in every exchange. Speaking openly and honestly about what matters most—your needs, boundaries, ideas, and decisions—builds trust and alignment in every area of life. These conversations strengthen relationships with your team, clients, and family by blending kindness with clarity.

## Exhausted Explorer™

One of three Middle Zone leadership types. An Exhausted Explorer is deep in the Middle Zone, surrounded by trees with no clear view of the path below her or summit above her. She feels trapped in a cycle of exhaustion, constantly reacting to urgent demands and struggling to gain control of her time and vision. She often feels disconnected from her original goals, overwhelmed by decisions, and burdened by tasks she shouldn't be handling. She worries about losing all the success she's built, yet continuing to run the business in the same way feels just as risky—maybe more so. If she keeps on this path, overwhelm, resentment, and burnout will only get worse. To break free, she needs to bravely press pause, take a strategic step back, reassess priorities, regain clarity, and restructure her leadership approach to prioritize decision-making, delegation, and strategy over day-to-day firefighting.

## Impossible Freedom™

When you feel fully lit up in business and life—*and* drive more financial growth at the same time. You're no longer in the zero-sum struggle of feeling you must sacrifice your life for your business or your business for your life. It's the breathing room beyond the Middle Zone, where success no longer demands overwork, time guilt, and decision fatigue. You have the space to lead, live, and thrive—where your time is fully yours, your impact is limitless, and your business fuels your freedom rather than consumes it. You have more time, energy, and joy while climbing to never-before-seen business success and personal fulfillment.

## Impossible Freedom Equation™

Ascend Leadership Co.'s proven leadership model that helps you climb out of the Middle Zone and ascend to Impossible Freedom. You reclaim your time, unite your team, and grow your revenue so you can live a deeply fulfilling life *and* drive financial growth at the same time. The equation includes the two Leadership Pillars and three Leadership Amplifiers:

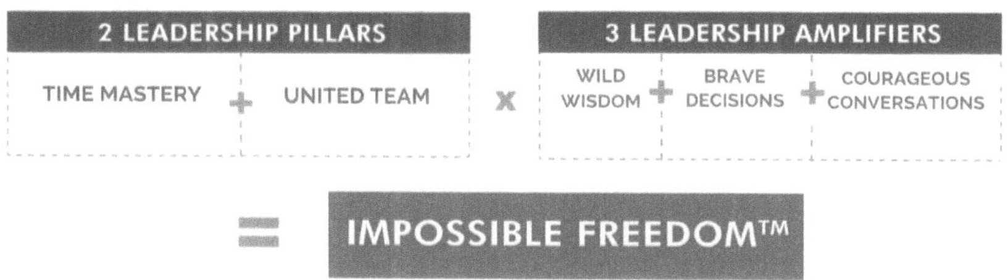


This isn't about doing more or working harder. It's about leading yourself, your time, and your team differently. Your time is yours again. Instead of being trapped in back-to-back meetings, you're finally in control of your schedule. Your team is engaged and optimized. They don't just wait for your direction; they lead alongside you. You make more money with ease, not exhaustion. Your business runs at a high level, without running you into the ground.

## Impossible Freedom Executive Leadership Coaching Program™

Ascend Leadership Co.'s signature executive leadership coaching program that guides high-achieving founders and CEOs out of the Middle Zone to successfully ascend to Impossible Freedom. You learn how to simultaneously reclaim your time, unite your team, and make braver leadership decisions rooted in self-trust, so you can feel fully lit up in business and life—*and* drive more financial growth at the same time.

## Impossible Freedom Quiz™

A five-minute diagnostic tool that reveals your Middle Zone leadership style, biggest Time and Team Leaks, and next best step to drive both business growth and personal freedom. Take it here: ascendleadership.com/quiz.

## Middle Zone of Success™ or Middle Zone™

The space between the success you've built and the freedom you crave. A plateau where your business looks impressive from the outside but costs you too much personally on the inside. It's the hidden trap of success without freedom—a plateau filled with overwork, time guilt, and decision fatigue. Staying stuck in the Middle Zone leads to resentment, exhaustion, and burnout.

## Momentum Builder™

One of three Middle Zone leadership types. A Momentum Builder is a high achiever making steady progress but facing inefficiencies that slow her down. She has a clear vision but struggles with subtle misalignments in time and team management, such as over-involvement in decisions, hesitancy to delegate, or unclear team roles. While she's on a clear path, these inefficiencies risk compounding over time, leading to slower growth, more stress, and unexpected obstacles. To move forward, she must refine her leadership approach and optimize her strategies before these leaks become major obstacles.

## Natural Genius™

What you're naturally best at, most passionate about, and what drives more revenue. It's the unique intersection of your strengths, passions, and revenue-driving activities that allows you to lead with clarity and ease, rather than burnout and overextension.

## Overworked Climber™

One of three Middle Zone leadership types. An Overworked Climber is gaining altitude, but it's getting harder to breathe. She's experiencing growth but at the cost of her energy, decision-making clarity, and personal freedom. She's caught in a cycle of working long hours, constant problem-solving, and an overwhelming workload, which drains her ability to think strategically. Without intervention, she risks burnout, reactive decision-making, and becoming the bottleneck in her own business. Her next step is to identify and eliminate hidden workload burdens, such as decision fatigue and delegation resistance so she can transition from survival mode to sustainable success.

## Talk with Ascend™

A no-cost personalized clarity session with Nadine and Derek Nicholson designed to help you break free from the Middle Zone and uncover the most important next step to take back your time, energy, and joy while unlocking never-before-seen success. Book your call here: ascendleadership.com/talk.

## Say/Do Gap™

The disconnect between what you say you value and how you actually spend your time. The Say/Do Gap shows up when your calendar is full of obligations but leaves no room for the people, priorities, and pursuits that give your work meaning. You say freedom matters, yet your schedule keeps you tethered to execution instead of vision. This gap fuels resentment, burnout, and time guilt—and closing it is the first step toward Impossible Freedom.

## Support Gap™

When your team isn't yet operating at the level that truly frees you. It's the disconnect between having people in place and feeling supported by them. The Support Gap appears when delegation is inconsistent, roles are misaligned, or accountability keeps bouncing back to you. Even with strong talent, you still feel like you're holding everything together. It keeps you stuck in the weeds, managing instead of leading, and limits how far your business can grow. Closing the gap means building a team that moves mountains with you, not one that adds to your load.

## Team Leaks™

When gaps in team alignment and support drain your focus and momentum in the Middle Zone. Team Leaks show up as skill misalignment, fragmentation, or leadership leaks, creating patterns that leave you carrying more than your share of the load. The result is inefficiency, missed deadlines, and stalled growth while you remain the bottleneck. Closing Team Leaks empowers you to build a United Team that plays to its strengths, communicates with clarity, and shares ownership for sustainable success.

## Time Leaks™

When inefficiencies in how you use your time drain your energy and growth in the Middle Zone. Time Leaks show up as time guilt, overworking, and overthinking—patterns that keep you stretched thin, second-guessing yourself, and unable to be fully present. Instead of fueling intentional growth, your days are consumed by firefighting, long hours, and decision fatigue. Even rest feels elusive, as your mind is relentlessly pulled in multiple directions. Closing Time Leaks means reclaiming time as a source of freedom rather than a zero-sum game where you always feel behind.

## Time Mastery™

One of two Leadership Pillars. Bold, unapologetic alignment between what you say matters most and how you actually spend your time. Time Mastery means designing your days with intention so your schedule reflects your values and highest-impact priorities, not just urgent demands. It's about taking ownership of your time from the inside out, focusing your energy on what you do best so you stay lit up, renewed, and prioritized. Instead of letting external pressures dictate your pace, you create space for what truly matters. The result is your time becomes a source of freedom, fueling both business success and personal fulfillment.

## United Team™

One of two Leadership Pillars. A cohesive, empowered support system that drives your vision forward and frees you to lead strategically, not manage reactively. United Team means surrounding yourself with the right people (employees, partners, mentors, advisors, and family) who share your mission, contribute meaningfully, and help you lead at the level you're meant for. When your team is aligned and engaged, they carry more of the load, creating sustainable growth for you and your business.

## Wild Wisdom™

One of three Leadership Amplifiers. The leadership strategy of trusting your inner knowing (your spirit, intuition, and embodied awareness) so you lead with clarity and self-trust instead of fear. Wild Wisdom reconnects you to your inner compass, helping you move from overthinking to alignment. Being outside in nature is a shortcut to this inner compass. By tuning into the deeper wisdom held in your heart and gut, you can make decisions with confidence, conviction, and calm, even in uncertainty.

# IMPOSSIBLE FREEDOM IN ACTION

**The Middle Zone (Chapter 1)**

"Before working with Nadine and Derek, things were very stressful. I was overworked, worn out, and feeling I should just throw in the towel and retire. I was trying to keep all the balls in the air: running the business, meeting client needs, and trying to keep my team motivated.

The business was doing well, but I was at a low point. I had been running my business for a long time and didn't realize how stuck I was. I was physically stressed, feeling burned out, and concerned my health was slipping. I didn't know if it could be different, and I didn't have a lot of faith that it could be different. I just felt stuck and didn't know what to do.

Nadine and Derek told me things could be different and saw a vision for me that I couldn't. They gave me hope that there was a different way of doing things. They helped me be more intentional and have the courage to dream bigger than I thought I could.

It was uncomfortable at first because my negative self-talk kicked in, like, *Who do you think you are? You can't do this. You'll never do that.*

And lo and behold, with their help, my big dreams actually became my reality. Nadine and Derek helped me shift my focus, reclaim control of my time, and finally build a business that worked for me instead of running my life.

I now show up with more power, enjoy my business again, and get the right results from the right efforts. My dreams didn't just stay ideas—they became reality. Looking back, I'm not sure I'd still be in business if I had kept going the way I was.

Nadine and Derek have tools and systems that are proven and work. They were really good at understanding my strengths and how I worked. They customized their tools and systems for me and my business. They always had my best interests in mind in whatever they said and did. I trust them wholeheartedly."

**—Rachelle Lee**
Einblau & Associates

"I have more freedom and spaciousness in my life than ever before, and my profits continue to increase. I was stuck in the Middle Zone, constantly working harder for diminishing returns and sacrificing my personal time to keep up. With Nadine and Derek's help, I completely restructured my work rhythm. Now I rarely work after hours, spend more time with my family, and my revenue has doubled—after years of only seeing a 10 percent increase. I'm a better leader, mother, and business owner, and for the first time, I truly trust myself, my team, and my decisions."

**—Jen Zagorsky**
Bright HQ Organizing Co.

## Time Guilt (Chapter 2)

"Before meeting Nadine and Derek, I used to think it was normal for my business to overtake my life and to lie awake worrying in the middle of the night. Every time I turned off my computer, I felt guilty that I didn't get enough done that day. When I was with my family or focused on myself, I felt guilty that I should be working. I felt completely drained and stuck in a cycle I couldn't break.

I knew I needed to make a change and could not continue as I was. Nadine and Derek helped me see that I had put me on the back burner, and it was taking a toll on my business, my family, and my health. I was surprised how quickly we got results. The process was seamless, and I felt the value right away.

With their help, I took control of my time, reconnected with my passion, and completely shifted how I lead my business and my team. I saw meaningful business growth while also regaining control of my time and curing the time guilt I was feeling. I'm leaps and bounds ahead of where I was before—healthier and happier and showing up in more control and at my best in the different areas of my life."

**—Katie Phillips**
Tricon Solutions Inc.

### United Team (Chapter 3)

"Derek brings a calm, structured approach that makes even the biggest leadership challenges feel solvable. His ability to simplify operations, align teams, and eliminate leadership bottlenecks helped me make major shifts in how my team and I run my business. With his support, I was able to make tough hiring decisions, unite my leadership team in the vision for my new role, and empower our leaders to excel. They work together to solve problems to at least the 90 percent level and develop new opportunities, bringing them to me for insights and approval of the final solutions. I can maintain oversight without getting bogged down in the day-to-day operations while we are experiencing even greater success for the company."

**—Anne Staines**
Sagent

"How have I operated and led my business without Nadine and Derek until now? I honestly can't imagine it at this point. I am so beyond grateful to have the two of them in my corner on my team. They have an authentic and inspiring way of guiding me toward the next version of myself in all facets of my business and life. I am so thankful I showed up at that conference in Phoenix and met Nadine, making one of my most important connections ever."

**—Stef Tschida**
Ripplea

"Before working with Nadine and Derek, I was spread too thin, overwhelmed, and constantly in the weeds of my business. I needed balance, stronger leadership, and a team that could take more ownership. After working together, I've completely redefined how I lead, set strong boundaries, and empowered my team—giving me the time and energy to focus on my biggest legacy project yet. With their help, we also solved major operational pain points and brought in a large amount of outstanding revenue. The results happened fast, and the process was seamless."

**—Gretchen Lambert**
Studio 2LR

## Wild Wisdom (Chapter 4)

"Nadine and Derek are a beautiful blend. Nadine is like Mother Earth and makes it safe to be yourself. She quickly gets to the heart of the matter and supports you in and through the unknown to new possibilities. I love Derek's analytical mind. He is supportive, clarifying, and draws out your inner wisdom. I now have a deeper trust in myself and the steady path from within rather than getting swept away by the flash and the quick-and-easy. You will be surprised at how simple it actually is to make more money with them while getting your life back. It's only halfway through the year, and we've made more than all of last year, I've worked less, and I'm having more fun and time with my family."

**—Dawn Ross**
Bit by Bit Bodyworks

## Brave Decisions (Chapter 5)

"Before working with Nadine and Derek, I was stuck in survival mode, modeling the same burnout behaviors I saw in my team. I knew something had to change but wasn't sure what. Nadine and Derek helped me step back, realign my leadership, and create a healthier, more sustainable path for my business and my life.

Now I make strategic decisions with confidence, knowing I have the clarity, tools, and support to build the future I envision for myself, my team, and my family. I no longer feel guilty about investing in my leadership. I see now that taking care of myself isn't indulgent; it's necessary.

If you're thinking about coaching but unsure if it's the right investment—trust me, it is. I never thought I needed a coach, but working with Nadine and Derek has changed the way I lead, the way I make decisions, and the way I show up in my business and life. Their support has been invaluable."

**—Susie Quesada**
Ramar Foods

## Courageous Conversations (Chapter 6)

"As someone with a PhD in English, a professional writer, and a well-published academic, I consider myself an expert in communicating thoughts, ideas, and concepts clearly. But one of the most valuable aspects of working with Nadine has been her ability to help me prepare for Courageous Conversations with my team, our clients, and my family.

Nadine offered me language I wouldn't have thought to use on my own, and she helped me approach high-stakes situations with more ease and less fear. When I was overwhelmed or overthinking, she brought clarity, practicality, and a sense of lightness. Her support was invaluable not only for my business, but also for my personal life, especially with several pivotal conversations I had with my sisters after our mother's death. This is no small thing. Her coaching and guidance to have Courageous Conversations shifted the direction of my life and my business more than once.

Having a skilled, unbiased professional communicator in my corner—someone who could walk me through what to say, how to say it, and sometimes even giving me the precise phrasing to use—profoundly impacted the quality of my life and my future."

**—Laura Bush**
Peacock Proud Press

## Ascended Possibility and Self-Leadership (Chapter 7)

"Before working with Nadine and Derek, I thought success meant working harder, putting in more hours, and constantly chasing growth. But I was stretched thin, struggling to step into the next level of leadership, and unsure how to scale without burning out. Nadine and Derek helped me trust my instincts, reclaim my time, and make bold decisions that actually moved my business forward. I stopped chasing incremental wins and started leading with more clarity and confidence. The impact? I cut 15 full workweeks from my schedule while more than doubling my revenue, and I recently started taking Fridays off to focus on me. I'm now growing my business sustainably in a way that fuels my freedom, and I don't need to kill myself hustling and grinding to do it. I get to be an example of growing a business in a sane, healthy way."

**—Stef Tschida**
Ripplea

### Defying Can't (Chapter 8)

"Before working with Nadine and Derek, I was heading toward burnout. Sales were higher than ever, but my ability to deliver was crashing. In just seven days, they completely transformed my calendar, cutting clutter and inefficiencies while creating a service model that allowed me to scale without overwhelm. Within thirty days, I had a clear path to quadruple my revenue, build a team, and create a work rhythm that felt both luxurious and sustainable. It was like lifting the weight of the world off my shoulders."

**—Julie Cabezas**
Self Made

### Living in Freedom and Legacy (Chapter 9)

"I used to believe that working less meant sacrificing business growth. Nadine and Derek help me cut my working hours by 75 percent *and* have our most profitable year ever. I am proud to say that I am functioning for the first time in the history of the company as a true CEO. Sagent is healthy and no longer a day-to-day worry for me. Nadine and Derek delivered on everything they said they would."

**—Anne Staines**
Sagent

# ACKNOWLEDGMENTS

### FAMILY

**From Nadine to Derek:** Derek, you are my rock, my steady ground, and my safe place to land. You keep me grounded while helping me soar.

When I feel lost, you bring me back to my center with your calm presence and unwavering clarity. You see what I can't see, hear what I'm not saying, and guide me with patience and love.

You teach me that leadership is about trusting the process, leading with integrity, and believing in what we're building together. Your humble strength, your analytical mind, and your heart-centered wisdom make everything we do better, stronger, and more united.

You teach me that asking for support is the bravest thing I can do and that the greatest gift we can give each other is permission to be human.

I couldn't climb this mountain without you. I wouldn't want to. I love you.

**From Derek to Nadine:** You are a force of nature—fierce, intuitive, and unstoppable.

You see straight to the soul of things, cutting through limitations and illuminating what's truly possible with a clarity that takes my breath away. You've taught me to trust my heart as much as my head and to lead from a place of deep inner knowing instead of fear.

Your courage inspires me every single day: the way you make Brave Decisions without apology, rooted in your inner Wild Wisdom; the way you have Courageous Conversations while being both kind and firm; and the way you protect what matters most—our family, our values, our freedom—with the fierceness of a mama bear and the wisdom of Mother Earth herself.

You are my partner in all things. I love you beyond measure.

**To Keane:** The moment you were born, everything changed. We thought we knew love, but you cracked our hearts wide open, and we've felt a depth of emotion we didn't know existed. You help us know with conviction what truly matters in this lifetime.

You teach us more about leadership than any book ever could. That showing up matters more than achievement. That integrity means keeping promises to the people we love. That the greatest legacy we'll ever leave isn't this book or our business—it's you.

Watching you grow into this wise, grounded, clear-eyed young man fills us with awe. You know who you are in a way that took us decades to learn ourselves. Watching you and your cat Kwasii play with each other fills our hearts with love.

We hope someday when you hold this book in your hands, you feel us beside you, reminding you that you get to have a life that lights you up, your dreams don't require permission, and the time to live is always now.

We are so incredibly proud of you. We adore you, and we'll be in your heart always and in all ways.

## To Nadine's Family

**To my mom, Marge:** You've shown me what loving strength looks like. Through every challenge, every loss, every moment that tested you, you keep going with grace, love, and resilience. Thank you for teaching me to be fierce and tender all at once, for modeling what it means to protect what matters most, and for always believing in me. You are the sweetest, kindest, most genuine, and generous person I know. I love you so much.

**To my dad, Paul:** I carry you with me every single day. You gave me my first Courageous Conversation in your final days. You taught me that Time Mastery begins with recognizing how precious and finite our time really is. Your passing showed me what truly matters. That final conversation by your bedside—where we each said all that needed to be said—changed the entire trajectory of my life. Thank you for that gift and thank you for teaching me not to wait for someday.

**To my sister Wanda:** When you left engineering to become a teacher and have more time with your kids, you showed me what a Brave Decision looks like in real life. As I watched you make that leap, something shifted in me. If you could defy the "can'ts" and reinvent yourself, so could I. You make me braver just by being brave yourself. You inspired the path I'm on today. I looked up to you then, and I still do now. You are a role model for me. Thank you.

**To my sister Elisa:** You are one of my greatest cheerleaders, standing beside me through every climb and celebrating every summit reached. You show me what it means to show up for the people you love, to celebrate their victories as your own, and to offer encouragement freely and generously. Thank you for sharing your wisdom, your compassion, and your encouragement. I know you've got my back, and it means the world to me.

## To Derek's Family

**To my dad, Jim:** You taught me about hard work and perseverance, and your example shaped my early understanding of what it meant to provide for a family. Thank you for the lessons, both the ones you intended and the ones that emerged through experience. Your influence is woven into who I've become. Thank you.

**To my mom, Del:** You held our family together through so much. Your quiet strength and resilience showed me what it means to keep going even when things are hard. Thank you for the love you gave, for creating a home, and for the ways you shaped me that I'm still discovering. You taught me more than you will ever know.

**To my sister, Des:** You called me "cold and unfeeling" once, and at the time, you were right. I had built walls so high I didn't even know they were there. But the truth you spoke helped me see what I needed to change. Thank you for your honesty, even when it was hard to hear. You helped me become someone who can now lead with both my head and my heart.

## MENTORS

**To Kelly Taylor:** You urged us to write this book when we couldn't yet see it ourselves. You helped us design a life where "work optional" became possible and where freedom was a strategic plan we could walk toward with confidence. You taught us that we are our number one asset. Your passing reminded us that the time to make the changes we've been putting off is always now. Not someday. Now. We miss you and will never forget you.

**To George Kansas and Tracey Trottenberg:** You changed the trajectory of our lives and our business in ways we're still discovering. Thank you for encouraging us to lead in nature and to trust what becomes possible when ambitious entrepreneurs step outside their offices. Thank you for being the coaches we needed at exactly the right moment. This book carries forward the inner Wild Wisdom you helped us unlock. We are forever grateful.

**To Gina Fink:** You were there before this work had a name. Your questions, coaching, and steady belief helped find language for what was being sensed long before it was clear. This book stands, in part, on the foundation you helped us build nearly two decades ago.

## CLIENTS

**To our clients:** You are the heartbeat of this book and the reason we do this work.

The stories in these pages come from your courage—your willingness to climb out of the Middle Zone of Success, your bravery in closing the Say/Do Gap and Support Gap, and your trust in us to guide you toward your personal vision of Impossible Freedom.

Your faith helped us build what Ascend has become. Your honesty and commitment inspire us every single day. Watching you step into the leaders you were meant to be fills us with awe. While you need to walk your own steps, you don't need to walk alone. We're honored to be your guides on the mountain and walk beside you on your path.

## THE ASCEND TEAM

**To Cara Wray:** Thank you for your commitment, reliability, consistency, and care. Your willingness to learn, to show up, and to be part of our team has played a meaningful role in bringing this book to life.

**To Dean Powell:** Thank you for nearly twenty years of financial guidance and support. You know our history, you understand our story, and you offer advice that is grounded in that understanding. You inspire confidence, keep us steady, and have been a trusted partner in bringing this book and our business to life.

**To Janet Pliszka:** You have been the photographer for our family and our business for fifteen years. You've seen us through every stage. You have a gift for seeing the light in people and bringing it out for the world to see. Your work captures who we really are, and we are grateful for you.

**To Laura Bush and Taryn Blanchard:** Laura, your brilliant mind, your gift with language, and your ability to see what we were trying to say made this book stronger, clearer, and more powerful. You challenged us to go deeper, to be braver, to trust that our message matters. Taryn, your meticulous eye and your care for every detail ensured that our message landed with precision and clarity. You caught what others would have missed and elevated the quality of every single page.

**To Lisa Haggis:** You are the architect of our brand, Ascend Leadership Co. From the beginning, you saw how to combine our individual strengths so we could serve clients more powerfully as a unified force. You invented the paradoxical "Impossible Freedom" and captured in two words what had taken us years to articulate. You saw the possibilities before we could, believed in us before we did, and gave us the language that became our rallying cry.

**To Pam Lavers:** You supported us through major decisions and helped shape the direction of our company. When Kelly passed away, you carried the weight of losing your life and business partner, and yet you continued to show up for your team and your clients. You care and you care big.

**To Sarah Milne:** Thank you for bringing our brand to life visually. You took the brand strategy and essence of Ascend and translated it into the visual identity that carries this work into the world. Your creativity and clarity helped shape how people experience our brand.

**To Tish Times:** Thank you for your commitment to helping us meet leaders who truly need what we do. At conferences around the world, you represent Ascend Leadership Co. with passion, authenticity, and unwavering belief. Thank you for championing Impossible Freedom with the same passion we feel and helping leaders find the path out of the Middle Zone toward the freedom they deserve.

**To Nadine's WPO Calgary III peers:** Thank you for your unwavering support, your fierce encouragement, and for standing beside me through the triumphs and the struggles. I adore you and believe in you. And a special mention to Dawn O'Connor. For more than twenty years, your influence has shaped my leadership—and my zero inbox. You are a masterful facilitator for the Women Presidents Organization, a wise guide, and a respected leader. Thank you for creating the conditions where women entrepreneurs can rise together.

**And to Mother Nature:** You are our wise teacher, our trusted guide, and our faithful companion.

In the forest, by the river, on mountain ridges, and along remote trails—you hold space for our deepest questions and whisper the answers we need most. When we feel lost, you bring us back to our inner truth. When fear clouds our vision, you clear the path with your stillness and presence.

From the sacred bench in the fog-draped forest where grief and gratitude met, to the towering cliffs of Kalalau where you declared yourself our co-facilitator, you show us that time with you is our number one life and business strategy.

You are the shortcut to our deepest truth, to our inner Wild Wisdom. The fastest path home to ourselves. Thank you for calling us back again and again to what matters most. For reminding us that we are you. This book is our love letter to you.

**Finally, to you, the one holding this book:** Thank you for picking up this book. We know you're carrying a lot right now: the weight of responsibility; the pressure to keep it all together; the inner voice asking if there's another way to lead and live that doesn't require constant personal sacrifice.

That voice? That's your Wild Wisdom. And it brought you here for a reason.

You may be deep in the Middle Zone, feeling trapped between the success you've built and the freedom you crave, or you may be standing at a crossroads, sensing that the strategies that got you here won't take you where you want to go. Either way, you're ready for something to shift.

We see you. We've been where you are. And we wrote this book to show you that Impossible Freedom is yours to claim.

The journey ahead will ask you to close Say/Do Gaps, build a United Team, make Brave Decisions, and have Courageous Conversations. It will challenge you to trust your inner knowing, to lead from alignment instead of obligation, and to choose presence over performance.

It won't always be comfortable, but it will be worth it.

Because you deserve a business that fuels your life instead of consumes it. You deserve to feel fully lit up while driving financial growth.

Not someday. Now.

Thank you for trusting us to guide you on this climb. We're honored to be part of your journey toward Impossible Freedom.

You're closer than you think. Aim higher, Powerhouse!

With deep respect and belief in what's possible for you,

**—Nadine and Derek**

# ABOUT THE AUTHORS

**N**adine Nicholson is a Master Certified Coach and an Accredited Business Communicator with degrees in public relations and psychology. She's also an alumna of Harvard Business School, 100 Women to KNOW in America, and member of the Women Presidents Organization, a global network of female leaders of multi-million-dollar companies.

Nadine built her career believing hard work was the price of success. She led large teams, earned international recognition, advised top executives, and managed multi-million-dollar operations. From the outside, it looked like achievement. Inside, she was working seventy-hour weeks, missing time with her family, and sacrificing her personal well-being for business growth.

Then everything changed.

A moment of clarity forced her to confront a truth: Success without being present with the people and experiences that bring joy isn't success at all. She walked away from corporate leadership and chose to redefine how leadership and life could coexist.

Today, as Co-Founder of Ascend Leadership Co., Nadine works with seven- to nine-figure founders and CEOs to close the gap between success and freedom. Her work centers on Time Mastery, Courageous Conversations, high-stakes decision-making, and leading in a way that fuels growth without costing what matters most.

**Derek Nicholson** holds a degree in commerce from the Haskayne School of Business and is certified in Change Management and Facilitation. His experience spans healthcare, energy, and entrepreneurial firms, where he built high-performing teams capable of driving revenue independently.

Over forty years in leadership development, business scaling, and sales strategy taught Derek a critical lesson: Businesses stall when everything depends on the leader. He has seen high achievers overextended, buried in day-to-day execution and carrying responsibilities their teams were capable of holding.

As Co-Founder of Ascend Leadership Co., Derek helps seven- to nine-figure founders and CEOs close the Support Gap by building teams that operate with clarity, accountability, and confidence. Known for his calm, analytical approach, he simplifies complex challenges into practical systems that work.

Together, Derek and Nadine are award-winning entrepreneurs who love hiking, biking, and golfing in the Rocky Mountains.

If this book surfaced something in you, trust it. Start a conversation with us at ascendleadership.com/talk.

Ready to see where freedom and growth aren't fully aligned? Explore your next step at ascendleadership.com/quiz.

Nadine and Derek are available for speaking opportunities. Check out their signature talks at ascendleadership.com/speaking.

* 9 7 8 1 9 5 7 2 3 2 3 2 4 *